# Facing the Facts

## The Truth about Sex & You

STAN & BRENNA JONES

*A NavPress resource published in alliance with Tyndale House Publishers,*

NavPress is the publishing ministry of The Navigators, an international Christian organization and leader in personal spiritual development. NavPress is committed to helping people grow spiritually and enjoy lives of meaning and hope through personal and group resources that are biblically rooted, culturally relevant, and highly practical.

**For more information, visit NavPress.com.**

*Facing the Facts: The Truth about Sex and You*



A NavPress resource published in alliance with Tyndale House Publishers



The Team for the Third Edition:

Don Pape, Publisher
Heather Maryse Campbell, Developmental Editor and Copy Editor
Jennifer Ghionzoli, Designer



For information about special discounts for bulk purchases, please contact Tyndale House Publishers at csresponse@tyndale.com, or call 1-800-323-9400.

Cataloging-in-Publication Data is available.

ISBN 978-1-63146-948-0

Printed in the United States of America

27 26 25
9 8 7 6

# FACING THE FACTS

TO JENNIFER & BRIAN

# CONTENTS

# ACKNOWLEDGMENTS

**WE OFFER HEARTFELT THANKS TO** the many parents who have shared their stories and perspectives, praise, and disagreements about the content of the five-book God's Design for Sex series as we have spoken and taught about this subject around the country and around the world. Some of your stories have made it into the revised versions of these books!

We remain thankful for our friends mentioned in previous editions, with whom we shared the joys and travails of the journey of parenting our young children through to adulthood and with whom we shared enriching dialogue about the ideas in this book. Continuing thanks also to thirteen generations of graduate students in Stan's Human Sexuality summer course (1983–95), whose insightfulness, openness, and inquisitiveness so enriched our understanding of sexuality, and whose stories of how they learned (or mostly not) about sexuality in their families were an inspiration for these books. Revisions to the second-edition children's books were enriched by the professional reviews of Steve Gerali and Elaine Roberts; special thanks to Susan Martins Miller for her editorial expertise on that edition.

As we prepare the third edition of these books, there are many whose help we are grateful to acknowledge: We owe special thanks to Wheaton College for its support of the scholarship of its faculty, particularly in the form of a spring 2017 sabbatical. Stan was encouraged in 2011 by the opportunity and invitation by the editors of *Christianity Today* to share the essence of our approach in the pages of that important journal.[1] Emily Verseveldt served as an outstanding graduate research assistant 2014–15, gathering and updating a great deal of material for the *How and When* book; Emily, you are a model of organization and resourcefulness. Thanks also to Amy Smith, who has served as Stan's research assistant since 2017 and provided additional research and critical proofreading. Dr. Glynn Harrison, professor emeritus of psychiatry at

University of Bristol, gave us the enormous gift of his review of and suggestions for the entire five-book series, for which he has our everlasting gratitude.

Each of our children's books benefited greatly from the editorial wisdom of Cathy Davis (for the original versions), Susan Martins Miller and Elaine Roberts (for the second edition), and, most lately, Caitlyn Carlson (for this third edition). Thanks to Steve Gerali for his careful review of the first edition of *Facing the Facts* and to Keith and Dawn Hartsell, and Peter and Elizabeth Hubbard for their thoughtful comments on the current revision. Special thanks for their careful review of the entire *Facing the Facts* revised book manuscript to Dr. Ted Witzig Jr., his daughter Coreena, and his professional colleague Brian Sutter at Apostolic Christian Counseling and Family Services. Ted, the Holy Spirit certainly prompted your continuing involvement.

We are pleased to welcome Dr. Mark and Lori Yarhouse as current reviewers and future collaborators on this book series. Stan had the honor of contributing to Mark's training in clinical psychology at the master's and doctoral levels at Wheaton College, and together they have coauthored a number of articles and books. Since leaving Wheaton, Mark has established a distinguished career as perhaps the most prominent Christian psychological researcher in human sexuality in the world. Lori has invested her energies with Mark in parenting and homeschooling their three children. Our intent is that they will progressively become more involved with future revisions of the series. No one deserves deeper thanks than the Yarhouses for their extraordinarily helpful review of the entire five-book God's Design for Sex series in both the second and third revisions.

Special thanks to our NavPress editor, Caitlyn Carlson, and the publisher of NavPress, Don Pape, for your wisdom, friendship, and tremendous support. We are grateful as well for the partnership between NavPress and Tyndale House Publishers.

Finally, we want to express our deep love, appreciation, and pride for our three (now adult) children. Thank you for being our initial living laboratory for working out these ideas, for the shape and texture of your lives today, and for being so thoughtful, strong, and loving. Thank you for the wonderful spouses you brought into our family, whom we love as our own children, and for our dear grandchildren. You have, together and individually, enriched our lives far beyond what we ever could have imagined.

# AN IMPORTANT WORD TO PARENTS

*General Introduction to the God's Design for Sex Series*

**PARENTS, GOD GAVE YOU** your sexuality as a precious gift. And you're reading this book because God has given you a child you love as a gift flowing from your sexuality.

God gave your child the gift of sexuality as well. If handled responsibly, this gift will be a source of blessing and delight. How can parents help make this happen?

Many forces will push children to make bad choices about sex based on false beliefs and values and on misplaced spiritual priorities. These forces are more powerful, confusing, persuasive, and ever present today than ever in history, thanks to the power of social media and the confusion of our culture. From their earliest years, children are bombarded with destructive, misleading messages—messages about the nature of sexual intimacy, about marriage, about family, about the boundaries of godly sexual expression, and even about the basic creational design of humanity as male and female.

These messages come from everywhere—through music, television, the Internet, discussions with their friends, school sex-education programs, and many other sources. The result? Confusion, doubt, and shame, as well as distressing rates of sexual experimentation, teen pregnancy, abortion, sexually transmitted diseases, divorce, and devastated lives.

We believe that *God means for Christian parents to be their children's primary sex educators.* First messages are the most powerful—why wait until your child hears distorted views and then try to correct the misunderstanding? Sexuality is a beautiful gift—why not present it to your child the way God intended? God's Word is trustworthy and true—why not teach your child how to understand and live by its guidance in the area of sexuality? Why not establish yourself as the trusted expert to whom your child can turn to hear God's truth about sexuality?

The God's Design for Sex series is designed to help parents shape their children's character, particularly in the area of sexuality. Sex education in the family is less about giving biological information and more about *shaping your child's moral character.* The earlier you start helping your child see himself or herself as God does, including in the area of sexuality, the stronger your child will be as they enter the turbulent teenage years.

*How and When to Tell Your Kids about Sex* is a parents' resource manual in which we offer a comprehensive understanding of what parents can do to shape their children's sexual character. The four children's books in this series are designed for parents and children to work through together. Those books are structured to be read with your child at ages three to five (*The Story of Me*), five to eight (*Before I Was Born*), eight to twelve (*What's the Big Deal?*), and twelve to sixteen (*Facing the Facts*). These age ranges are not strict formulas; you need to exercise your judgment about your child's maturity level, environment, needs, and so forth to decide when and how to introduce the books.

The four children's books are meant to provide the foundational information kids need. Further, they are to be starting points for you to build upon and personalize as you discuss sexuality with your child in an age-appropriate manner. They provide an anchor point for discussions in order to jump-start deeper explorations. These books help break the silence and put the issues out on the table.

Don't simply hand these books to your child to read, *because our whole point is to empower you as the parent to shape your child's sexual character.* The books are meant to start and shape conversations between you and your child and to deepen your impact on your child in the area of sexuality.

In this series, we address controversial topics about which Christians disagree, including masturbation, how far people should go sexually when they're dating, contraception, gender identity, homosexuality, and more. Our goal in doing so is not to presumptuously present our answers as completely right but rather to encourage you to reach reasoned conclusions and to teach your child as you see fit before the Lord.

We have tried in each book to present information that we believe children of that age must have, without presenting controversial topics "too early." Your child may be confronted with complicated and confusing issues at a much earlier age than you expect. In such cases, you can draw on our discussions in later books to inform your dialogue with your child. For instance, we hold off on discussion of sexual orientation until the book for eight-to-twelve-year-olds (*What's the Big Deal?*), and on discussion of gender identity and transgender issues until the book for twelve-to-sixteen-year-olds (*Facing the Facts*). But your child may need more basic information much earlier, and in such cases, we urge you to use or adapt material from this book and our books for older children to meet your child's needs.

Why start early? Because if you as the parent are not teaching your child about sexuality, your child will learn distorted lessons about sexuality from television, the Internet, and playground conversations. If you are silent on sex while the rest of the world is abuzz about it, your child will learn that you cannot help in this key area. If you teach godly, truthful, tactful, and appropriate lessons about sexuality, your child will trust you more and see you as a parent who tells the truth.

We'll briefly unpack each of the books at more length to help you discern which would be most helpful to you in your current parenting season.

PARENT RESOURCE

### *How and When to Tell Your Kids about Sex:*

*A Lifelong Approach to Shaping Your Child's Sexual Character*

This book is the parents' comprehensive resource manual for the God's Design for Sex series. We take on the hardest subjects, such as sexual abuse, gender identity, and homosexuality, helping you know when and how to bring up these subjects. Our goals for *How and When to Tell Your Kids about Sex* are to

- help you understand your role in shaping your child's character, including his or her views, attitudes, and beliefs about sexuality;

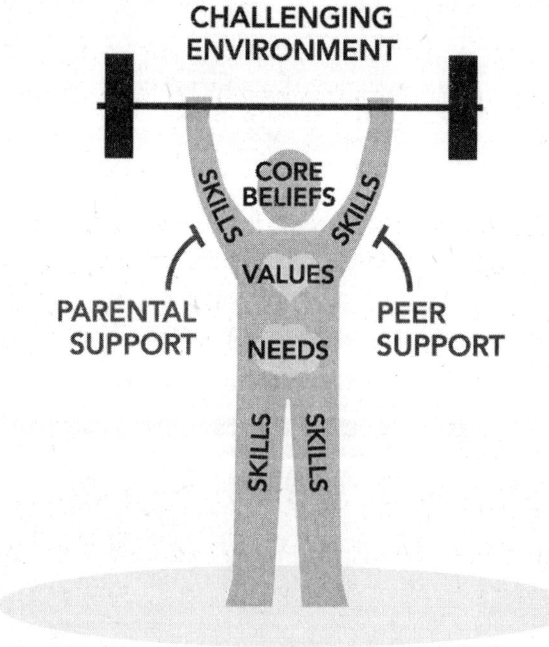

- instruct you in the twelve key principles for Christian sex education in the home and how to implement the strategies and tactics suggested by these principles;
- familiarize you with the challenges that your child will face from secular culture and empower you with strategies and skills to help them overcome those challenges;
- ground your understanding of God's view of our sexuality;
- equip you and your child to explain and defend the traditional Christian view of sexual morality in these modern times;
- examine each major developmental stage of your child's life and share age-appropriate information and approaches;
- address directly the most complex issues you and your child might or will face in today's culture in a manner grounded in biblical thinking and informed by the best contemporary science;
- explore how you can most powerfully influence your child to live a life of sexual chastity; and
- equip you to provide your child with the strengths necessary to stand by their commitment to traditional Christian morality.

As you read the following descriptions of each of the books for your child, please know that the concepts and issues presented in each of these books flow directly from the background provided by this foundational parents' guide.

#### AGES THREE TO FIVE

### *The Story of Me: Babies, Bodies, and a Very Good God*

Your most important task with your young child is to lay a spiritual foundation for their understanding of sexuality. God loves the human body (and the whole human person), and the body is included in what God called "very good" (Genesis 1:31). Children's bodies, their existence as boys or girls, and also their sexual organs are gifts from God.

Young children can begin to develop a wondrous appreciation for God's marvelous gift of sexuality by understanding some of the basics of fetal development. In this book, we discuss the growth of a child inside a mother's body and the birth process. With such instruction, young children begin to develop a trust for God's law and to see God as a lawgiver who has the best interests of his people at heart. God is the giver of good gifts!

Finally, we want children to see families grounded on the lifelong marital union of one man and one woman as God's intended framework for the nurture and love of children. If you are reading the book as a single parent or with an adopted child, you will have opportunity to talk about how God sometimes creates and blesses alternative forms of families. We hope that you will find *The Story of Me* a wonderful starting point for discussing sexuality with your young child.

### AGES FIVE TO EIGHT

**Before I Was Born:** *God Knew My Name* by Carolyn Nystrom, with Stan and Brenna Jones

*Before I Was Born* emphasizes the creational goodness of our bodies, our existence as men and women, and our sexual organs. This book introduces new topics as well, including the growth and changes boys and girls experience as they become men and women.

It includes a tactful but direct explanation of sexual intercourse between husbands and wives. God wants sexual intercourse limited to marriage, because sexual intercourse brings husbands and wives close together in a way that honors God and helps to build strong families.

Parents often ask, "Do my kids really need to know about sexual intercourse this early?" Remembering that you are the decision maker as to whether you use this book with a very mature five-year-old or with a more slowly maturing eight-year-old, the answer is yes. We believe this is a strategic decision parents must face based on their individual children, considering that first messages are always the most powerful messages. If, as a Christian parent, you want to begin to shape a godly attitude in your child about sex, why would you wait until they first soak in the misperceptions of the world? Why not build godly attitudes and views from the foundation up?

If you're reading this with an adopted child, use this opportunity to explain that not every couple will have biological children. If a baby doesn't grow in the wife's womb, the couple might look for a baby to adopt. And some women are not able to take care of a baby, so another family might adopt the baby and make it part of their family forever. Even though the baby grew inside a different mother, the husband and wife love this baby very much. Adoption is another way that God makes families.

### AGES EIGHT TO TWELVE

### *What's the Big Deal?: Why God Cares about Sex*

This book reinforces the messages of our first two children's books, covering the basics of sexual intercourse and the fundamental creational goodness of our sexuality. It continues the task of deliberately building children's understanding of why God intends sexual intercourse to be reserved for marriage.

This book goes further than the earlier books, adding more of the facts your child will need to know as they approach puberty. Further, it will help you begin the process of inoculating your child against the negative moral messages of the world. In *How and When to Tell Your Kids about Sex*, we argue that Christian parents should *not* try to completely shelter their children from the destructive moral messages of the world. If they mature in environments where they are not exposed to germs, children grow up with depleted immune systems that are ineffectual for resisting disease. When parents shelter their children too much, children are left naive and vulnerable; parents risk communicating that the negative messages of the world are so powerful that Christians cannot even talk about them.

But neither should you let your child be inundated with society's destructive messages. The principle of inoculation suggests that you should deliberately expose your child to the contrary moral messages they will hear from the world. It should be in your *home* that your child first learns that many people in our world do not believe in reserving sex for marriage, and it should be in your home that your child first understands such problems as pornography, teenage pregnancy, gay marriage, sexual identity and gender issues, and so forth. In this way, you can help build your child's defenses against departing from God's ways.

#### AGES TWELVE TO SIXTEEN

### *Facing the Facts: The Truth about Sex and You*

*Facing the Facts: The Truth about Sex and You* builds upon all that has come before but also—in more depth—prepares your child for puberty. At this age, your child is old enough for more detailed information about the changes their body is about to go through and about the adult body they will soon receive as a gift from God.

In this book, your child will hear again about God's view of sexuality and about his loving and beautiful intentions for how this gift should be used. The distorted ways in which our world views sex must be clearly labeled, and your child must be prepared to face views and beliefs contrary to those they learn at home. We attempt to do all this while also talking about the many confusing feelings of puberty and early adolescence.

While children could read this book independently, we do not believe this would be optimal. We encourage you to read it alongside your child and then talk about it together. You could go chapter by chapter. Alternatively, you can read it and use it as a resource for important conversations with your soon-to-be or young teenager.

In this book, we address the most controversial topics of the series, topics about which biblically grounded Christians can and do frequently disagree. We make suggestions about appropriate moral positions on all of the important issues, including sexual-intimacy limits before marriage, masturbation, contraception, gender identity, homosexuality, and more.

We have joked that in each of these books, we are guaranteed to say something to lead almost any Christian parent to declare us too conservative or too liberal on some topic or to disagree with us somewhere. We do not presume our answers are completely right. At the very least, we hope our thoughts empower you, the parent, to think the matter through and present a better answer to your child as the Lord guides your thinking.

All of these books were written as if dialogue is an ongoing reality between mother, father, and child. Yet in some homes, only one parent is willing to talk about sex. Many Christian parents shoulder the responsibility of parenting alone due to separation, divorce, or death. Grandparents sometimes must raise their grandkids. We've tried to be sensitive to adoptive families and families that do not fit the mold of the traditional nuclear family, but we cannot anticipate or respond to all the unique needs of families. Use these books with creativity and discernment to meet the needs of your situation.

We hope these books will be valuable tools in raising a new generation of faithful Christian young people. If you follow this plan, we believe your child will have a healthy, positive, accepting, godly attitude about sexuality. As an unmarried person, your child will be more likely to live a confident, chaste life as a faithful witness to the work of Christ in their heart. If your child does marry, we believe they will have a greater chance of having a fulfilled, loving, rewarding life as a husband or wife. It is our prayer that this curriculum will encourage and equip you to dive into the wonderful work of shaping your child's sexual character.

PART 1

# *Getting the Big Picture!*

## CHAPTER 1

# *Different Stories, Different Lives*

Zoe can't wait to grow up. As long as she can remember, she has looked forward to being an adult, having the responsibilities and freedoms of an adult, having a grown-up body, and moving on to whatever God has in store for her.

Adam, on the other hand, wishes he wouldn't grow up. He's happy just as he is. He loves his friends; he loves to play. He feels as though everything in his life is just the way it should be, and he sees no good reason why his childhood should end.

HOW DO YOU feel about growing up? Are you excited or worried? Most of us have a mixture of good and bad feelings about growing up. It's hard! All mothers and fathers have experienced at least some of the same feelings you're having, though it's hard for some to remember—and even harder to talk about.

Almost all adults asked the same questions you may be asking: "Why is this happening? Why is God doing this to me? What will it be like to be an adult with an adult's body? What is sex? What is it for, and what does it mean?"

These are good questions. And depending on what you choose to believe about your life as a whole, the answers to them can be very different. There are many different ways for us to understand our lives. Each life is rather like a story, and sex is part of each.

Let's imagine the possibilities as four basic stories. You're moving steadily down the highway of life, and ahead of you are four different exits—four different paths to choose from. Each gives answers to the deepest questions of life, questions such as the following:

- Where did the world and everything in it—including me—come from?
- Is there purpose in life?
- Is there anything special about being a human being?
- Are truth, beauty, and goodness real?
- Is love real? And what does sex have to do with love?

Your decision about which story to believe and to live by has real consequences for your life. Let's hear from four people—each one represents one of the four views.

## BAILEY, THE BOLD MATERIALIST

"Sure, I can answer those questions. The first answer is 'We don't know why the world exists or where it came from. We can't ever know.' The other answers are 'No, there's no purpose, we're nothing special, and all those things like love and beauty are just labels we put on feelings. They're not real things—they don't really exist.'

"Look, scientists agree on one thing: All that there is anywhere is energy and matter. That's all that exists. We're just a complicated bunch of atoms that take human form until we die—then it's over. There's nothing else—no god, no reason, nothing. The universe happened by pure chance, life happened by pure chance, evolution happened by chance, and billions of years later, here we are.

"People imagine they have a special 'purpose' because they're too afraid to admit that it's all just the result of chance. They make up a god and other stuff like love because they're afraid to be realistic.

"The thing that comes closest to being a purpose is the instinct we feel to perpetuate life. Evolution builds into our genes the need to survive and breed. That's why there's sex. All the rest that goes along with it—love, beauty, etc.—is just an illusion. Sex is just the way for my genes to get into the next generation and beyond."

### TAYLOR, THE INWARD SEEKER

"Wow, Bailey, did you ever miss the point! Yes, the universe happened, and yes, life has evolved over billions of years. But something special happened in the universe: Somehow, something bigger than just energy and matter happened.

"Human beings are part of that. We've evolved to sense and reach for something beyond the material world. We can grope toward something true, real, and purposeful—even if that something is different for each of us.

"These differences are okay because each of us is basically good. Each of us has a special spark we can find by looking inside ourselves. We must look beyond the mere physical to find our true selves. We should be seeking and defining our real selves—that's what life's about! You don't find your true self by following rules others create—you live true to yourself.

"Sex sometimes means you love someone—but it can also mean you like them, you just want to have fun with them, or whatever. As long as no one is hurt, no one is forced to do something they don't want to do, and everyone is playing fair, then anything goes.

"Some people think everyone is either male or female, but that's too limited. Our true selves aren't defined by others or even by our bodies—we're defined by the 'inner Me.' Some people are girls trapped in boys' bodies, some are boys trapped in girls' bodies, and some people are something else—whatever they choose to be."

### RYAN, THE RELAXED CHURCHGOER

"Taylor, you're right that Bailey is missing some things, but so are you. God must be real, because otherwise the universe doesn't make any sense.

"I happen to be a Christian because I grew up that way, but there's not just one path to God. Jesus was a good teacher. I think he was the best teacher and the one who understood God the best, but all the major religions say basically the same things in different words. I think God loves us and wants us to find that inward spark you talked about. God wants us to be our true selves, and the teachings of Jesus can help us do that.

"God wants us to love others and be good. God means sex to be something special, an expression of love. Some fanatic weirdos get all hung up on the tiniest details of what the Bible says, but we have to use common sense to figure out how it applies today.

"Because sex is an expression of love, we should be careful with it. We should feel something strong before we share our bodies with people. Certainly love can be just as real between two men or two women as it can be between a man and a woman.

"People who love each other can get married, but they don't have to as long as they're loving and committed. A wedding is just one way to be faithful. And in an overpopulated world, the choice to have a baby is a serious one. Every woman should have the right to stop a pregnancy if she's not ready to have a child."

### JORDAN, THE JESUS-FOLLOWER

"I agree that there's something real beyond the physical universe. I see beauty that's real and good, but I also see a lot of ugliness. I think we have yearnings for higher purpose for our lives. We believe goodness and justice exist—but there's a lot of evil in the world and in us. And we know there's truth—but it's often clouded by distortion and falsehood.

"The early Christians who wrote the Bible believed that God revealed himself perfectly in Jesus. If this God made people in his image, then it makes sense for us to see beauty, purpose, goodness, and truth—because God is all of those things.

"Jesus is widely admired, but if you read the Bible, you're confronted with a dilemma: Jesus was more than a nice guy. The Bible presents him as doing miraculous things and making outrageous claims about himself, such as that through him we could 'not perish but have eternal life' (John 3:16) and 'I am the way, and the truth, and the life. No one comes to the Father except through me' (John 14:6).

"The most outrageous part of the story is that after Jesus died a horrible death on the cross, he rose from the dead in victory over all sin and evil. The lives of the apostles prove they really believed their claims: This defeated, discouraged group became dynamic leaders who changed the world. Of the eleven original apostles who stayed faithful, ten died by brutal execution and one died in isolated banishment, all for their faith.

"I follow Jesus, God's eternal Son, so I can have purpose, meaning, and eternal life. Because I believe in him, I believe my life should be understood and lived as he would want me to, according to his teachings.

"Through the Bible, we're taught that sex is a special gift and part of what it means to be made in God's image. If we use the gift of sex rightly, we have the best chance to experience real, faithful love that gives us joy and brings us closer to God."

Which story is closest to the one you believe makes sense of your world? Which will you choose? If your perspective is similar to that of Jordan, Jesus' follower, or even if you're undecided but open to this view, then we invite you to think with us about sex as Jesus does.

In this book we expand on Jordan's words about sex being a gift from God. We talk about the realities of how your body will change and about the very different choices young men and women make about sex because they're living by different stories.

Our most important goal is that you understand God's view of sex, because we believe that during this critical period when you're physically becoming an adult woman or man, you can begin to understand that sex is a bigger, better, more lovely gift than you ever realized.

Let's get started.

## CHAPTER 2

# *God Gives the Gift of Sex*

**GOD MADE EVERYTHING.** That means that God made sex. He made men and women with sexual bodies capable of having sexual intercourse (intercourse is commonly referred to as "having sex," but in this book we use the word *sex* to mean our differences as sexual men and women as well as the act of intercourse). Is sex something dirty that God made grudgingly? Should we feel ashamed about sex?

Is it possible that our sexuality is important in more ways than we think? Is it possible that sex is close to the center of God's purposes for the world? Is it possible that it's badly misunderstood today?

In this chapter we talk about the gift of sex, and in the next chapter we look at what sex means to God.

### WHO DO YOU THINK YOU ARE?

As we wrote those words above, we could imagine someone saying, "Who do you think you are to say what God thinks? Only fanatics think they speak for God! There are many different opinions about God's view of sex!"

We do not think we speak for God. But here's the thing: We *do* believe in and follow Jesus. For two thousand years, Christians have believed the following:

- Jesus taught and acted in a way that shows us he believed that what we now call the Old Testament was God's Word.

  "Do not think that I have come to abolish the Law or the Prophets; I have not come to abolish them but to fulfill them. For truly, I say to you, until heaven and earth pass away, not an iota, not a dot, will pass from the Law until all is accomplished." MATTHEW 5:17-18

- Jesus believed that his own words were on par with Scripture. (For example, when he said things like "You have heard that it was said _____, but I say ______.")

  "All things have been handed over to me by my Father, and no one knows the Son except the Father, and no one knows the Father except the Son and anyone to whom the Son chooses to reveal him." MATTHEW 11:27

  "You have heard that it was said to those of old, 'You shall not murder, and whoever murders will be liable to judgment.' But I say to you that everyone who is angry with his brother . . ." MATTHEW 5:21-22

- Jesus declared his own words to be eternal and completely reliable, to be the words (or Word) of God.

  "Heaven and earth will pass away, but my words will not pass away." MATTHEW 24:35

- Jesus taught his apostles that he would continue to speak his Word through his people, and so Christians came to believe that the writings of the early apostolic teachers that were assembled as the New Testament are Scripture.

> "There are some things in them [the writings of the apostle Paul] that are hard to understand, which the ignorant and unstable twist to their own destruction, as they do the other Scriptures." 2 PETER 3:16

*Who do we think we are?* We believe the Bible is God's true message to us all. For years we have read the Bible to understand what it says about sex, we've read what the best theologians and biblical scholars believe the Bible teaches, and we've looked at what the church has taught consistently about sex.

> All Scripture is breathed out by God and profitable for teaching, for reproof, for correction, and for training in righteousness, that the man of God may be complete, equipped for every good work.
> 2 TIMOTHY 3:16-17

We want to give you our best understanding of what God has said in the Bible about sex. So let's talk about sex!

### THE BEGINNING

Sex was God's idea. In the beginning, after God made everything else—sun, moon, stars, mountains, sky, plants, birds, fish—God made a man and a woman. Sex was very much a part of creation before God made people: There are male and female plants, fish, birds and bees, and beasts—all these living things reproduce through some form of sexual uniting. The Bible says God told nonhuman living things to "be fruitful and multiply" (Genesis 1:22)—that means sex.

But sex was and is special for humans. At the end of the first five days of Creation, God looked out on what he had made and saw that it was "good." That included the sexuality of all living things.

But on the last day of Creation—the day on which he made

man and woman as his final act—God saw that it was "very good" (Genesis 1:31). The creation of man and woman was like frosting on the cake of Creation.

> So God created man in his own image, in the image of God he created him; male and female he created them. And God blessed them. And God said to them, "Be fruitful and multiply and fill the earth and subdue it, and have dominion over the fish of the sea and over the birds of the heavens and over every living thing that moves on the earth." . . . And God saw everything that he had made, and behold, it was very good.
>
> GENESIS 1:27-28, 31

It's important to realize what this means: God was happy with the way he designed people as sexual beings. God looked at Adam—his genitals, his ability to become a father, and everything that was unique about him as a man—and God was delighted with what he had made. God looked at Eve—her genitals, her ability to carry a baby inside her body, her breasts to nourish that baby, and everything else that was unique about her as a woman—and God was very pleased with what he had made.

The Bible says that "the man and his wife were both naked and were not ashamed" (Genesis 2:25). Adam and Eve were delighted when they looked at each other. They felt no embarrassment, no guilt, and no need to hide anything. They knew they were made for each other. They were different from one another—just as all women are different from all men—and they knew those differences were something to celebrate.

**Genitals:** *the male or female sexual organs that can be seen between the legs*

**Sexual intercourse:** *what many people call "having sex" or "making love"*

It was God's idea that Adam and Eve would be able to have sexual intercourse as husband and wife. In fact, God made their bodies so that this would be loving and pleasurable and fun for them. It was God's design that they be able to have children because they had sexual intercourse. That was his plan for populating the earth.

God is happy that he made you a sexual being with a unique brain, a unique body, unique genitals, and everything else that goes along with your being a young man or a young woman. One of God's main purposes for the changes ahead for you is to complete the work of transforming you from a child into an adult.

## ADAM HAD IT MADE

You know the story. God made Adam first and put him in the Garden of Eden to take care of it. Adam had the perfect job in the perfect place with a perfect relationship with God. If there was ever anyone who should have been just fine alone, Adam was that guy.

But something was missing. God looked at Adam and said, "It is not good that the man should be alone; I will make him a helper fit for him" (Genesis 2:18). By "helper," God did not mean a servant—he meant a partner and companion for the man, someone whose life would be knit to the man's.

God made people with the longing for someone to share their lives with. When people are children, the love of their families can satisfy them. This is what families are meant to do. But when children become adults, they want something more—adults want special relationships with special people who are just for them.

In Genesis 2:20-23 the Bible says that after Adam looked at all the animals and saw that there was no partner suitable for him, God made Eve and brought her to him. Adam was so excited about this wonderful gift from God that he cried out, "This at last is bone of my bones and flesh of my flesh; she shall be called Woman, because she was taken out of Man."

## TWO BECOMING "ONE FLESH"?

The writer of Genesis went on to say, "Therefore a man shall leave his father and his mother and hold fast to his wife, and they shall become one flesh" (2:24).

"One flesh." What a beautiful way to describe the kind of relationship God wants in a marriage blessed by him! A powerful desire to be one flesh with another is planted deep inside every person's heart. God wanted it to be that way.

No one fully understands what becoming one flesh means, but we know at least three important things about it:

1. God's ideal for one flesh is for a man and a woman to exchange vows of marriage to each other before their families and their community, to express their love for each other by sharing their bodies fully with each other by having sexual intercourse, and to be open to the possibility of having children.
2. Though the man and the woman continue to be individuals, when they marry they're now more than individuals. They are a new thing: a unique family created by the union of their lives.
3. That's the ideal, but in the Bible, we read the apostle Paul's teachings that even the most casual and ugly type of sex—for instance, a man having sex with a prostitute—results in those two people becoming one flesh in some way. Sexual intercourse has this power. But it's clearly not the full thing, because Paul didn't say that every man who has sex with a prostitute is married to that person—he said that both of them have dishonored God and harmed their bodies and souls.

> Do you not know that your bodies are members of Christ? Shall I then take the members of Christ and make them members of a prostitute? Never! Or do you not know that he who is joined to a prostitute becomes one body with her? For, as it is written, "The two will become one flesh." But he who is joined to the Lord becomes one spirit with him. Flee from sexual immorality. Every other sin a person commits is outside the body, but the sexually immoral person sins against his own body. Or do you not know that your body is a temple of the Holy Spirit within you, whom you have from God? You are not your own, for you were bought with a price. So glorify God in your body.
>
> 1 CORINTHIANS 6:15-20

So God made sex—both the differences between men and women and sexual intercourse (commonly called "sex")—as a good gift. God told Adam and Eve that they as separate individuals would become one flesh by having sex in marriage.

But what does sex mean to God? What does it and should it mean to you?

CHAPTER 3

# *The Meaning of Sex in God's Story*

**GOD IS CHANGING YOU**, causing your body to grow from a child's body into an adult's body. He's graciously doing so to prepare you for the possibility—whether it happens or not—of becoming one flesh with somebody. When all goes according to God's plan and design, an adult longs to be united with a special person of the opposite sex in a lifelong love relationship.

If you don't have those feelings yet, you probably will within the next few years. You will feel ready to fall in love. And only when your body becomes a sexually mature adult body can you have the kind of relationship where you will be "glued together" into one flesh with your husband or wife.

Not everyone gets married. Single people can live in a way that honors God and allows them to have vibrant and full lives without spouses and without having sex. Whether God blesses you with marriage or with a single life, he has an important purpose for your life.

## YOU COULD BE A MODEL

In the last chapter, we talked about God's intentional creation of us as two basic kinds of human beings: male and female. He also gave the first married couple, Adam and Eve, the gift of sexual intercourse. But why did he do this?

God quite explicitly tells us why: He wanted to create beings "in his own image" (Genesis 1:27). But how does this answer the question?

The word *image* had a clear meaning in the ancient world (these words were written about four thousand years ago). The ancient Jewish people were surrounded by large and small kingdoms where people worshiped their own god or gods. The kings typically declared themselves to be children or special representatives of their gods. The kingdoms would put carved stone or wooden images of their kings or their gods (or both) around to stake out their territories.

Most of these ancient societies had a creation story, and almost all of these stories told of how the kings were direct descendants of the gods. The message was that the kings and their families were divine—the rest of the people were like cattle, slaves, or worker bees. They were considered nobodies.

> So God created man in his own image,
>     in the image of God he created him;
>     male and female he created them.
>
> GENESIS 1:27

The one true God revealed to his people a creation story that turned such pagan stories completely on their heads. How? By revealing that it was not just kings but all of humanity that was made in the image of God! This revolutionary statement revealed that we're all part of the royal family—we're all of divine descent.

The first of the Ten Commandments (see Exodus 20) says that you should worship no god except the true God. Have you ever wondered why the second great commandment says that God's people should never make a "carved image"?

Inferior images of wood or stone are forbidden because God gave us much more accurate and beautiful images: each other. Images made of stone or wood can only deceive us. God made his own best image by creating every human being in the image of God.

But what does this have to do with sex? We get hints of the answer throughout the Bible, hints through which God reveals a great mystery.

The Bible teaches that marriages between Christians are meant to be models of the way Christ loves his church. There are many places in the Bible where the time when God welcomes his people home to heaven is described as a wedding feast. It's a joyous celebration when the husband-to-be (Jesus) finally gets to marry the bride he loves (all those who believe in Jesus).

God wanted to put a model of this future right on earth so everyone could see the wonderful love he has for his people. That's one reason he made marriage.

Also, God hopes Christian husbands and wives will form loving, caring, committed relationships. If they do, people who don't believe in Jesus will be able to look at these marriages and say, "Oh, I get it! The love Jesus has for all of his people is like the love in that Christian marriage—just better and more perfect."

In a similar way, God has an important purpose for single people too. Jesus lived as a single person because his love and devotion were focused on God his Father and on all of us. The apostle Paul was also single. We read his words on the subject in 1 Corinthians 7:8: "To the unmarried and the widows I say that it is good for them to remain single, as I am."

Why is singleness a good thing? Because single people can model for others what it means to be totally faithful and dependent upon God, just as Jesus was.

### THE BIG MYSTERY!

But why are faithful Christian married people and single people singled out by God as such special models? And how does sex figure in?

We find out in the Bible that God is a Trinity—three in one and one in three. In the Trinity are God the Father, God the Son, and God the Holy Spirit. They are one divine being in three persons, eternally loving each other in total faithfulness. God is a united community so filled with love that he created human beings to share the infinite love within God the Trinity. The church has called this truth a "great mystery"—a truth that has been revealed to us by God, though we can only partially understand it.

Faithful Christian married couples made up of one man and one woman are God's special models to the world of the loving character of God the Father, Son, and Holy Spirit as a Trinity. The man and woman remain individuals while fully becoming one flesh (two in one and one in two). Their love can overflow in the creation of new life (their children) just as God's love overflowed in the creation of new life.

Faithful Christian single persons are God's designated models of the character of Jesus Christ. Jesus gave up the experience of the intimate love within the Trinity during the thirty-three years he spent on earth in order to share God's love with us and to demonstrate his love for the Father and Holy Spirit. God the Father poured out his love on his Son through the Holy Spirit. The single person relies on God and God's people for love and support in the same way.

### SUMMING IT UP

So why is God doing this to you? Why does your body have to change into a grown-up body? *It's part of God's plan for you.* He wants you to become the grown-up, sexual person he means you to be. He wants to give you a way to meet that deep hunger you will feel for a special relationship with a person who really loves you.

If you're blessed to marry someone of the opposite sex, he wants your marriage to be a model here on earth of his love for his people, and he wants to make it possible for you to have children. Should you remain single, he wants your life to be blessed, filled with the love of family, friends, church, and work. God wants you to show the world your love and loyalty to him by not misusing his gift of sex.

> "Therefore a man shall leave his father and mother and hold fast to his wife, and the two shall become one flesh." This mystery is profound, and I am saying that it refers to Christ and the church.
>
> EPHESIANS 5:31-32

## PUT AWAY YOUR FLASHLIGHT

Many people have mixed-up feelings about growing up and about sexuality. Stan was given a small book about sex when he was about your age. He was dying to know more about sex, but he felt ashamed and embarrassed for wanting to know—so embarrassed that he only read the book by flashlight at night when he was supposed to be asleep.

You don't have to do that with this book. It can be hard for parents and kids to talk together about sex. But even though it's hard, your parents gave you this book because they love you and want you to be able to understand this great gift of sexuality God has given you. Your parents can answer many questions you may have that we won't answer in this book.

Brenna, on the other hand, had the kind of relationship with her mother and father that allowed for easy and comfortable discussions about sex. It helped her look forward to growing up. If your parents aren't available for this kind of discussion, we hope you can find a trustworthy adult—maybe your youth leader in your church—who can frankly talk with you and answer any questions you have.

## WHY IS IT SO DIFFICULT?

What we have told you here is the truth about the origins, meanings, and purposes of sex. It's good news. Why, then, is the world so messed up about sex?

You probably know the story. Adam and Eve lived in a perfect world in which there was only one rule (and it was not a rule about sex). They rebelled against God, broke the one rule, and were expelled from their perfect world. All of us live with the mess they created—inside our lives and on the outside, too. The world around us is broken, and we're broken. We're often filled with shame, guilt, confusing or ugly desires, and selfishness.

But God sent Jesus to die for us so we wouldn't have to die. Jesus triumphed over death so we could have eternal life. All we need to do is ask for God's forgiveness and believe and follow Jesus. We follow Jesus by doing what he commands. And through our obedience to him, he can restore our sexuality to what it was always intended to be.

The world around us thinks the way of obedience is a narrow, prudish, tortured, or limited path. The world is wrong. The reality is that the way of obedience opens up possibilities of joy, freedom, and fulfillment that flow from living life the way God designed us to live. It's not always easy, but it's the way to an abundant life. God wants good for us.

PART 2

# *Understanding the Facts*

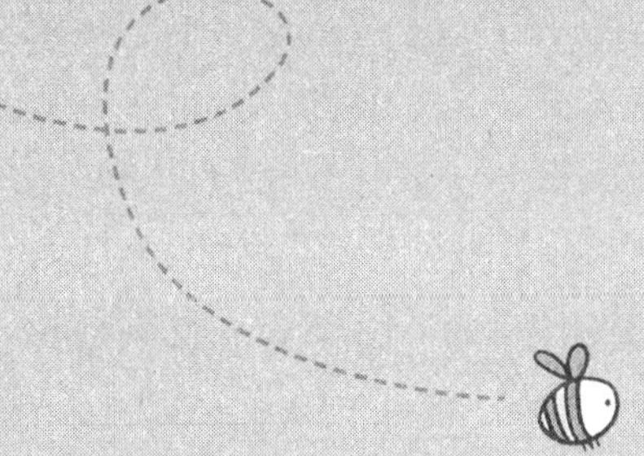

CHAPTER 4

# *How Women and Men Are Different on the Outside*

**BOTH BOYS AND GIRLS** go through growth spurts in puberty. Both get taller, heavier, and stronger. Both develop more and darker hair on various parts of the body, especially on the arms and legs. Both begin to develop pubic hair (the curly hair that grows just above the genitals). Many develop what doctors call acne: pimples and other skin problems caused by the excess oil the body produces during these changes. Similar as boys and girls are, though, there are important differences.

## OKAY, SO WHAT'S DIFFERENT?

In this chapter we focus on outward differences. We look at inner differences in the next two chapters. The most obvious outer difference between men and women is the difference between their genitals. Many people use slang words to describe genitals. We've heard of families who used the nonsense words "woo-woo" and "ding-ding" for the genitals. Perhaps some of you have used the word "wiener" or "peter" for a man's penis. Some words are not wrong, just silly and confusing. We once knew a woman who grew up calling her genitals the "in-between-the-legs"!

Some slang is dirty or rude—it takes what God made to be good and treats it as if it were evil. Some slang that men use to talk about women's bodies is insulting, either because the words are ugly or because they imply women's bodies are to be used by men. This is wrong.

Slang for body parts is often used when people are uncomfortable talking about sexuality and are nervous about using the correct words. In this book we use the words doctors use, unless the words are too complicated. Because God made our bodies and because sex was God's idea, we don't have to use slang.

## WHAT'S UNIQUE ABOUT WOMEN'S BODIES?

Girls and women have three openings between their legs that go up into the inside of their bodies. One is exactly the same as what men have: the *anus*. This is the opening that your bowel movements, or poop, come out of. The anus is in the crease between your buttocks in back.

Women have two other openings into the interior of their bodies: a *urinary opening* (where urine, or pee, comes out) and a *vagina*. These openings are hidden in the crease between the *labia* (which is Latin for "lips") between the woman's legs. When a young girl stands up in the tub to be rinsed off by her mom, all the mother can see of the girl's genitals are the two labia and the fold or crease between them. The labia are soft folds of skin padded with extra muscle and fat in a similar way to the lips on your face.

Right above the place where the crease between the labia stops is a soft bump called the *mons*. The mons is formed by part of the hip bone underneath the skin that has muscles attached to it, giving it a soft feel.

The name doctors use for all of a girl's outer genital structures together is *vulva*, which includes the mons, the labia, and the parts of the genitals between the labia that are not as readily seen. If your doctor ever talks about the vulva, he or she means this whole genital area. Some women just call this their genitals or their privates.

**Mons** *is Latin for "mound."*

The structures between the labia usually cannot be seen except when women deliberately spread their legs. Because the genitals of boys are on the outside and stick out a bit, and because boys handle their genitals when they go to the bathroom, boys are often more familiar with the way their genitals look than are girls. There's nothing wrong with a girl looking at the marvelous way God made her. But to do so, she has to bend and look or use a hand mirror.

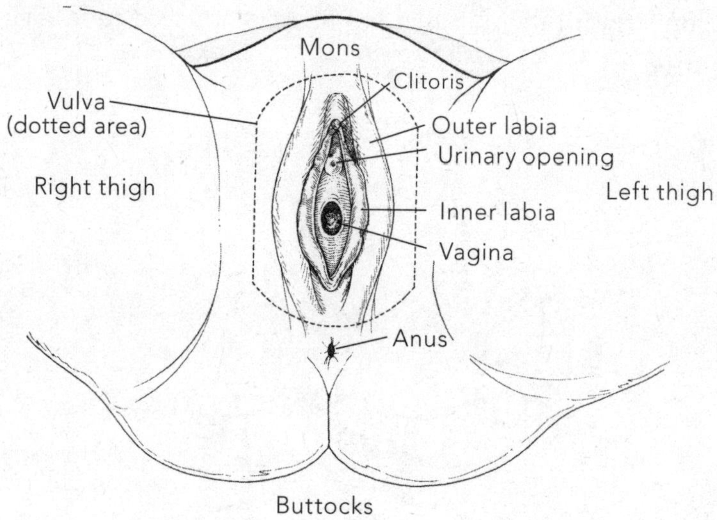


God placed four structures between the outer labia. One is easy to see on some women and not so easy to see on others. This is the inner labia or lips. These are loose folds of skin between the outer labia and the vagina.

Some women have smaller inner labia, while others have more tissue forming the inner labia, making them more visible. This is one way every woman is unique. The inner labia or lips have many nerve endings and are sensitive to touch.

*Doctors call the inner labia the* **labia minora**, *which is Latin for "minor" or "little"* (**minora**) *"lips"* (**labia**).

The woman's *vagina* is like a tube that goes inside the body for three or four inches. It is made up of muscles covered with tissue like the tissue on the inside of your mouth. This opening is smaller in many girls because of a piece of protective skin called the *hymen* that partially covers it. When a woman has sex, this piece of skin is broken or stretched.

*The* **hymen** *is a circle of skin that makes the opening of the vagina smaller and helps protect a girl's vagina as she grows up.*

In some parts of the world, the presence of the hymen is considered proof that the woman has never had sex, but this is not valid. Some girls are born with thick hymens, and some are born with hardly any. Also, hymens on many girls naturally stretch or break when a girl plays sports such as track or gymnastics.

God made the vagina for two things. First, it is the birth canal through which a baby comes out of a woman's womb. Usually the vagina is relaxed and somewhat closed, but amazingly it can expand so a baby's head and body can pass through.

*During* **childbirth**, *a woman's vagina can stretch to the size of a baby's head, which is about the size of a small cantaloupe!*

The other purpose of the vagina is to take in the husband's penis during sexual intercourse. The vagina has many nerve endings that help it feel good when the husband's penis moves back and forth in the wife's vagina during sexual intercourse. This would not feel good if the skin of his penis and her vagina were dry like the skin on your arm. For that reason, God made it so that when a wife feels excited about being close to her husband and making love to him (this is called being "sexually aroused"), her vagina makes a watery, slippery *lubrication* that makes it pleasurable to have sexual intercourse.

This lubrication doesn't happen only when you're married, however. After a young woman has developed an adult body, her vagina can become slightly wet when she thinks about an attractive boyfriend and begins to feel sexually aroused. This is normal and is not something to be ashamed of or feel guilty about. There's nothing wrong about feeling sexual excitement like this—you're simply responding as the sexual person God made you to be.

The third structure between the labia is the tiny opening through which urine comes out from the bladder. This urinary opening is located above the vagina (toward the mons).

The *clitoris* is the final structure between a woman's labia. The clitoris is a small bump above the vagina and the urethra, just below where the two labia come together. Of all the parts of the woman's genitals, the clitoris has more nerve endings and is more wonderfully sensitive to touch than any other part of her body. It seems that God made the clitoris for only one purpose: to give a woman pleasure from making love or being touched there by her husband.

Women and men respond basically the same way to the pleasure of sex. Husbands and wives both find that touching each other all over, but especially on the genitals, feels wonderful. So does having sexual intercourse. If this pleasure continues, it can get stronger and stronger. If the couple keeps giving each other pleasure, both the husband and the wife can have *orgasms*. An orgasm or climax is when the pleasure suddenly gets very strong and a person's body trembles a little all over. After an orgasm, a husband and wife usually feel very close to each other, with a sense of satisfaction and calm. Part of the joy of marriage is learning what gives your spouse pleasure and showing your love that way.

## WHAT ABOUT BREASTS?

Breasts of young boys and girls look alike. Both have nipples that are darker than the skin around them and breasts that are flat against the chest. But men's and women's breasts are quite different.

Adult women's breasts, no matter the size, have the same parts. The outside of a woman's breast is made of skin, with a nipple of darker skin at the center. The inside of a woman's breast has two parts: milk glands that connect to the woman's nipples through tiny tubes, and fatty tissue that makes her breasts soft. Women with small or large breasts have the same number of milk glands. The only thing that affects the size of a woman's breasts is the amount of fatty tissue in the breast. Breast sizes and shape vary from woman to woman.

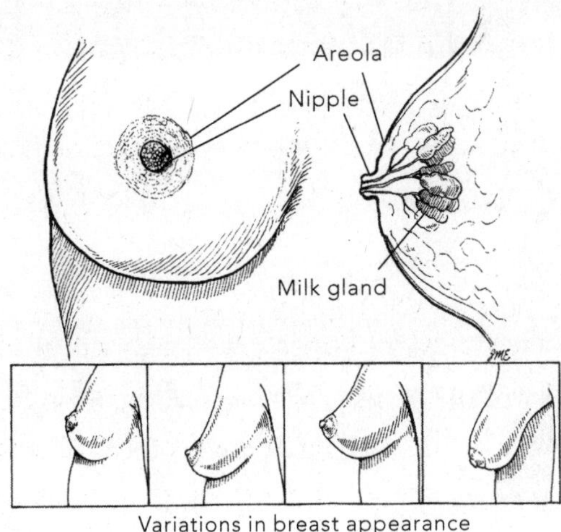


Variations in breast appearance

Women's bodies are a complex miracle. God made women in his image and blessed them with sexuality so they can enjoy beautiful sexual relationships with their husbands as well as the joy of pregnancy, childbirth, and nursing children.

## SO WHAT ABOUT MEN'S BODIES?

Just like women, in the crease between the buttocks, men have an *anus* for bowel movements. A man's genitals are easy to see. Most obvious is the man's *penis*. The penis has three main parts. First is the *shaft*, a soft, springy tube of tissue. The skin on the shaft of the penis is stretchy and doesn't have much hair on it.

The second part is the head or *glans* at the end of the penis. The skin on the glans is very smooth and sensitive, and the *urinary opening* through which he passes urine is at the end.

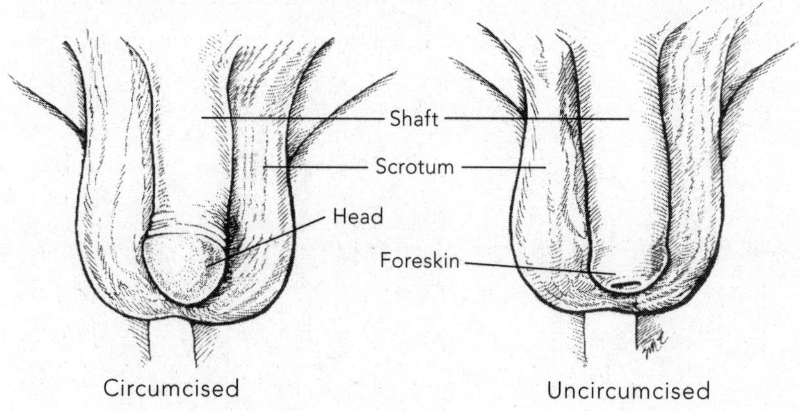


The third part of the penis is the *foreskin*, a continuation of loose skin from the shaft of the penis that covers most of the head of the penis of all baby boys. Some baby boys have most of their foreskin trimmed off soon after birth. This is called *circumcision*. Circumcision exposes the head of the penis. Between half and two-thirds of baby boys born in America are circumcised.

Customs about circumcision differ between cultures. For instance, most baby boys born to European and Latin American families are not circumcised. Jewish baby boys have been circumcised since the time of Abraham (see Genesis 17:10-14). Some early Christians argued that all Gentiles becoming Christians should be circumcised too, but the early church learned from God that this wasn't necessary (see Acts 15:5-21). So some Christians are circumcised and some are not.

Doctors disagree as to which is healthier, but men who have been circumcised find it a little easier to keep their penises clean. Men who haven't been circumcised should pull back their foreskins and carefully wash around the heads of their penises when they bathe.

Underneath the penis is a bag of skin called a *scrotum*. Right under the skin is a layer of muscle, and inside are the two *testes*. A boy can feel the testes when he touches his scrotum; they feel like two balls, so the common slang term for testes is "balls."

*The hormone that makes a boy into a man is called* **testosterone**.

**Sperm** *are tiny cells with whiplike tails that carry half of the genes needed to make a baby. The other half of the genes are in a woman's egg.*

The testes have two important jobs. First, they produce the hormone *testosterone*, a special chemical that changes a boy's body into a man's body and keeps him looking like a man throughout his life. Second, the testes produce *sperm*, which are essential for having children. The muscles of the scrotum move the testes closer to and farther away from the man's body to maintain the right temperature for the continuing production of sperm. When a boy is cold, the scrotum tightens, pulling the testes tight against the boy's warm body, but when a boy is warm, the scrotum loosens and hangs down so the testes can be cooler.

Like women, men are made in God's image, and their sexuality is a gift from God. Their bodies are made so they can enjoy sex and so they can become fathers. Let's celebrate God's great ideas!

## CHAPTER 5

# *The Changes Ahead for Girls*

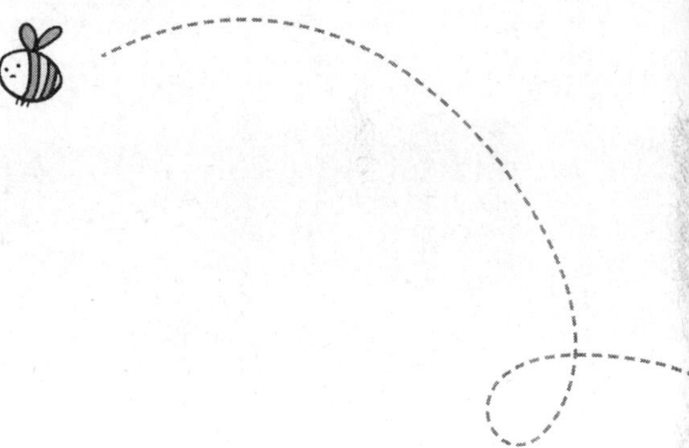

**SOMETIME BETWEEN** the ages of nine and fifteen, most often at age eleven or twelve, a girl's body begins to become a woman's body. Some girls' bodies start to change early, others late—everyone is different. Girls who start these changes early may feel odd and get teased for beginning to develop breasts or for growing so fast. Girls who go through the changes late might feel odd and get teased for looking younger than their classmates. God has different timing for different people, so try not to worry or feel that there is something wrong with you.

### THE INSIDE STORY

A woman's vagina goes up into her body for three or four inches. The vagina has an opening inside called the *cervix* that goes farther up

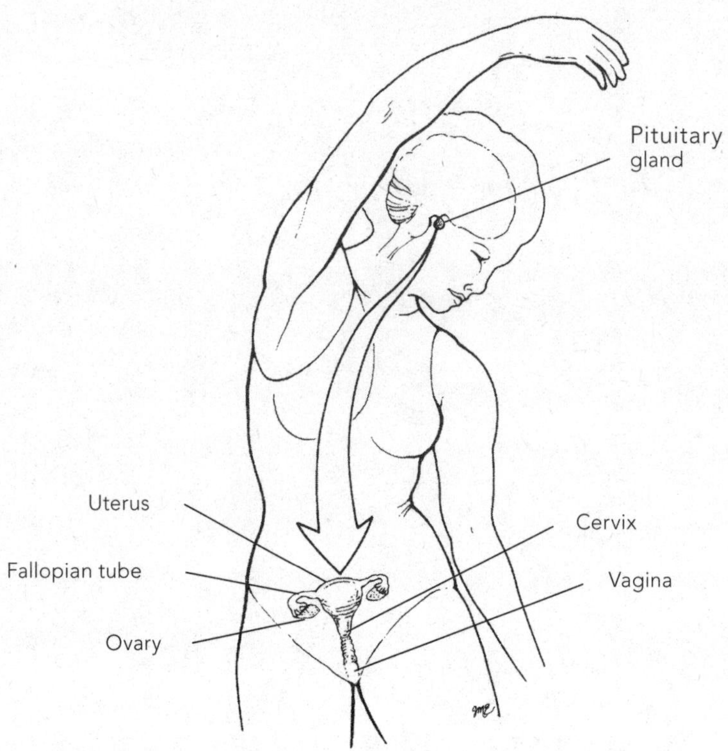


inside the body. The cervix is like a tiny doughnut with the hole in the middle squeezed closed. That hole opens into the woman's *uterus*, or womb. The cervix is the bottom part of the uterus.

The uterus is a muscular organ that provides a secure place for a baby to grow for nine months. It delivers the life-giving oxygen, food, and water the baby needs. The uterus is powerful enough to squeeze a baby out of a woman's body the way you squeeze toothpaste out of a toothpaste tube.

Normally, a woman's uterus is about the size of a closed fist. But by the time a woman is nine months pregnant and about to give birth, her uterus has expanded to almost the size of a small grocery bag big enough to hold a baby!

At the top the uterus branches out into the *fallopian tubes*, which lead from the uterus to the *ovaries*, one to the right and one to the left. The ovaries, like the man's testes, do two main things: They produce eggs (or *ova*; one egg is an *ovum*) and the hormones *estrogen* and *progesterone* that make a girl into a woman. The ovaries are located inside a woman's body on each side of a spot just below her belly button.

*The hormones that make a girl into a woman are* **estrogen** *and* **progesterone**.

*A woman's eggs or* **ova** *each carry half of the genes needed to make a baby. The other half of the genes are in a man's sperm.*

## PUBER . . . WHAT?

*Puberty* is an awkward and funny word that means the one-to-two-year time during which a person's body matures sexually. No one is sure how the body knows when to start puberty, but it's the brain's master gland, the *pituitary gland*, that signals a girl's body to begin puberty by sending chemical signals to the ovaries to release the hormones that cause her body to begin changing.

**Puberty:** *the time during which a child's body changes into an adult's body*

## WHAT HAPPENS FIRST?

The first change of puberty for most girls is that their breasts begin to develop. A young girl's nipple feels pretty much the same as the skin around the nipple. When breast growth begins, it starts as a little lump right underneath her nipple. Doctors call this lump a breast bud. For some girls the lump is very soft, and for others it's hard. A few girls experience a little discomfort or sensitivity in this area, but this usually doesn't last long. Over a period of two to four years or more, the breasts mature to their adult size through the growth of fatty tissue under the nipples and around the milk ducts. As in the rest of the body, this growth can come in spurts.

Breast development occurs at different rates for different girls and even at different rates in the same girl. For instance, many girls will notice one breast taking a couple of months to catch up with the development of the other. This can make finding a bra that fits well a challenge.

## IS BIGGER REALLY BETTER?

There is no "normal" breast size. Alyssa wishes her breasts were larger, while Laticia wishes hers were smaller. Breast size has nothing to do with a woman's ability to nurse a baby, because all women's breasts have the same number of milk glands and the same capacity to give milk. Women who have smaller breasts usually notice that their breasts are a bit bigger when they're nursing babies, but then their breasts go back to their previous sizes when they stop.

Because a woman's breasts have sensitive nerve endings, most women find it pleasurable when their husbands touch their breasts. This is a normal part of making love and expressing affection in marriage. The size of a woman's breasts makes little difference in how much pleasure she gets from having her breasts touched.

Sadly, some men think big breasts make a woman more attractive. Preferring women because of breast size is like preferring women with blue eyes to women with brown eyes—both are beautiful. Women can't do anything (besides surgery) to increase or decrease the size of their breasts (don't believe those ads for exercises, creams, or pills).

We urge you not to worry about breast size. Any man who considers breast size the determining factor for whether a woman is attractive isn't worth your time. Breast enlargement surgery has become a more common practice for women, but this seems a risky and extreme reaction to having smaller breasts.

About the time breast development starts, a girl's pubic hair begins to grow and her labia darken slightly in color. At first, pubic hair tends to be straight and fine. After several months, the hair becomes more curly and thicker. Women differ in the thickness of their pubic hair. Some have a very light growth of hair, while others have a lot of pubic hair. Just like breast (or nose or ear) size, this is a natural difference. Either way, girls may choose to remove some hair before wearing a swimsuit.

## BUT THAT'S NOT ALL

While her breasts are beginning to develop, a girl's internal organs and genitals change as well. The next big change is the start of her *menstrual cycle* or period, which usually occurs about twelve to eighteen months after her breasts begin to develop.

Typically, a woman experiences a menstrual cycle approximately every twenty-eight days. However, normal menstrual cycles may range anywhere from twenty-three to thirty-five days. The first few cycles of young women who are beginning to menstruate are often irregular and unpredictable, but later they become more regular.

For most women, the couple of days before menstruation begins are a time of mild discomfort. During this premenstrual time, a woman might notice some cramps in her stomach or feel a little more tired, grumpy, headachy, or down than usual.

Every woman is different. Some women don't experience this time before their periods as any big deal. But a few women have harder experiences and are diagnosed by doctors as having PMS or *premenstrual syndrome*. These women can experience symptoms severe enough to interfere with their lives—symptoms such as bloating and weight gain, mood swings, and sometimes even severe depression. If your symptoms seem extreme, talk to your parents about seeing a doctor.

When menstruation begins, a small amount of bloody flow passes from the uterus through the cervix and vagina. The flow is typically heavier on the first and second days of the menstrual period and then begins to slow down. Some women will have blood flow for only three days, and others will have it for up to six days. A woman's period can change from time to time, depending on her health, how much stress she is under, and other factors.

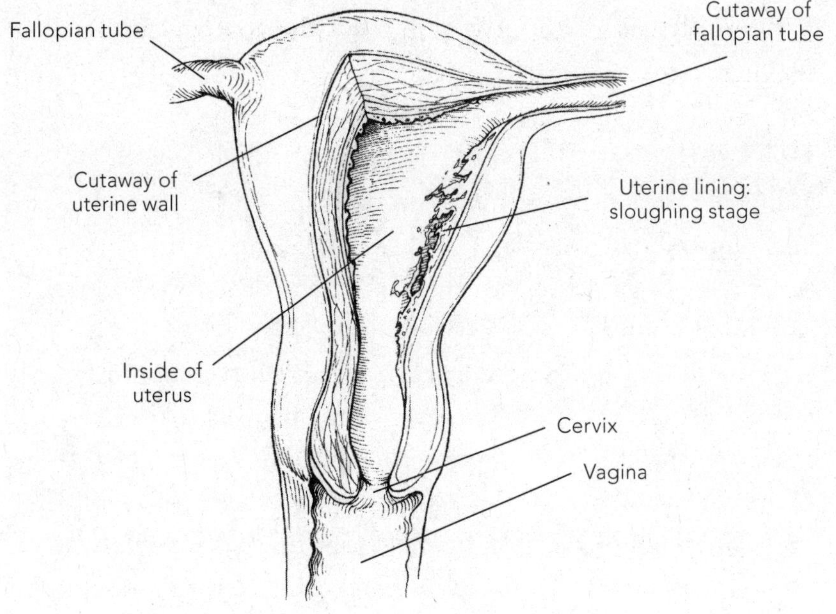


## WHY HAVE A MENSTRUAL PERIOD?

The reason for a menstrual period is tied to a woman's ability to get pregnant. Even when a woman isn't having sexual intercourse, her body still readies itself each month to get pregnant. To understand a woman's menstrual cycle, let's start with the very end of her menstrual bleeding.

During the ten to twelve days following the stop of menstrual bleeding, a woman's body prepares an egg to be released by one of her ovaries. As the time nears each month for her ovary to release the egg, her body rapidly prepares the inside of her uterus to nourish a baby in case that egg is fertilized and a child is conceived. That unborn baby will be nourished through the mother's blood in the extra-rich lining of tissue on the inside wall of the mother's uterus, where it would attach. Every month, the wall of the uterus has to build up this lining in order to be ready to nourish a baby.

The uterus holds its ready state for about a week, but if the woman is not pregnant, the rich lining of extra blood and tissue it just built up quickly dissolves. The menstrual flow that then comes out of a woman's vagina is actually blood mixed with tissue from the lining of the uterus. In this way, her uterus cleans out the unused preparation for pregnancy and clears the way for the next cycle.

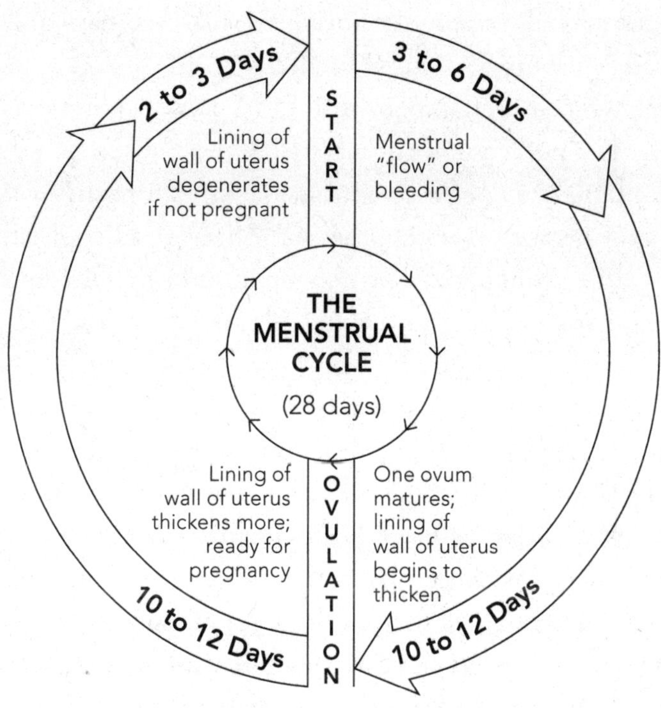


## WHAT IF I'M AT SCHOOL WHEN MY PERIOD STARTS?

It can be a little nerve-racking to know that your first period could come anytime twelve to eighteen months after your breasts begin to develop. Many girls don't feel confident that they'll know what to do when their periods start. *What if I'm in school? At a sleepover? Alone at home?* Most girls find out that they have started their first periods when, after a couple of days of feeling not quite right, they go to the bathroom and find some light red blood on their underwear or on the tissue when they wipe themselves.

Your parents can buy you some sanitary pads to keep ready for when your period begins. These are thin pads of cottony paper that soak up the menstrual flow and keep you clean. When you get your first period, change your underwear and begin wearing a pad that sticks to your underwear between your legs. Most women change their pads several times a day during the first two days of heaviest flow. Later they might change less often.

Some women use tampons instead of pads. A tampon is made of the same kind of absorbent material as the pad, except it's tightly packed in the shape of a small tube. A woman pushes a tampon gently into her vagina with either her finger or an applicator that comes with each tampon. The tampon absorbs the bleeding inside of the woman's vagina instead of letting it flow out. Inserting a tampon can be a little uncomfortable the first few times a young woman does it, but it doesn't hurt and quickly becomes as normal as wiping herself after she goes to the bathroom.

A tampon has a string that slightly hangs out of its user's vagina. Pulling on the string removes the tampon so it can be thrown away. Tampons must be changed regularly; not doing this can make you seriously ill. Depending on the heaviness of menstrual flow, tampons should be changed every three to eight hours during the day. You can put in a clean one before you sleep and change it when you wake. You should never leave a tampon in for more than eight hours.

Some girls experiencing their first periods aren't comfortable using tampons because they feel awkward about pushing something into their vaginas. Girls sometimes decide to use tampons because they want to do activities such as gymnastics or swimming that involve tight clothing or getting wet. Using pads or tampons is a personal choice you can talk over with your mother or another trusted woman.

Thinking ahead about your first period can help you not to be nervous. If your first period occurs at school, you can go to the school nurse or your teacher for help. If you have a male teacher, you can simply say, "May I see the nurse? I don't feel well." The school nurse will have pads on hand. If nothing else, you can fold a bit of toilet tissue into the crotch of your underwear until you can get a pad.

It can be helpful to keep track of your periods on a calendar to learn the rhythms of your cycle. When your cycle becomes regular, you can predict when you might begin your period and know when to carry pads or tampons with you. Some young women become regular within a few months, but some can have irregular menstrual periods for a year or more.

| | | 1 felt extra grumpy | 2 headache and some mild cramps | 3 began menstruating; took Tylenol | 4 same | 5 still menstruating, but not much |
|---|---|---|---|---|---|---|
| 6 almost stopped | 7 wore pad but no flow | 8 | 9 | 10 had an upset stomach | 11 | 12 |
| 13 | 14 | 15 | 16 | 17 | 18 | 19 |
| 20 | 21 | 22 | 23 | 24 had a headache | 25 false alarm! Feel all better | 26 |
| 27 | 28 | 29 a little headache, but not grumpy | 30 started my period | | | |

## A BLESSING OR A CURSE?

Women menstruate because God has blessed them by designing their bodies to prepare each month for pregnancies. Out of his abundant love, God created Adam and Eve. And then out of love, he sheltered them in the Garden of Eden. In the same way, a woman's body is a place for the creation and sheltering of new human life.

There is no one point when you stop being a child and become a woman, but having your first period is a clear signal that your body is becoming an adult body ready for pregnancy. This is the reason some mothers and families celebrate the first periods of their daughters. Your first period means you have made a big step toward adulthood, and that's something to be happy about.

Not all women feel good about their periods. Have you ever heard a woman describe her period as "the curse"? She may be among those few who have tough physical symptoms with periods, such as bad headaches or strong cramps. Even if your mother or older sister has these kinds of symptoms, that doesn't mean the same thing will happen to you. But if it does, you can talk to your mother and your doctor about how to relieve the symptoms of your period.

Some women feel that their periods are dirty, perhaps because the vaginal opening is close to the urinary opening and the anus. But God made the vagina to clean itself just as he made your eyes to clean themselves with tears. You've never washed out your eyes with soap, but you don't worry about them being dirty. Nor is the menstrual flow "diseased" or "bad" blood. It's no dirtier than blood coming from a cut on your arm.

One reason that some women think of their periods as dirty is that in the Old Testament God told the Jewish people (in the law of Moses) that women who were having their periods were unclean (see Leviticus 15:19-24). Does this mean God is disgusted by menstruation or that men should be disgusted with women who are menstruating? Absolutely not! Why, then, is this in the Bible?

In the Bible, the word *unclean* does not mean "dirty" in the way we use that word today: to refer to something full of germs and unhealthy to touch. Also, things that were unclean were not necessarily sinful. Most importantly, in the Old Testament God taught the Jewish people that *life* was found in blood, and life is special to God. For this reason, the blood of animals was used in sacrifices but was never eaten (kosher rules still require blood to be drained from any animal to be eaten).

These rules about blood helped prepare the Jews for God sending Jesus to die on a cross and shed his blood on our behalf. The Jews understood the preciousness of Jesus' blood and could comprehend that his blood was the final sacrifice to end all sacrifices. Once it was clear that the non-Jews (Gentiles) were welcomed into the family of God, God told Peter and his other followers that the things the Old Testament called unclean are no longer off-limits to us (see Acts 10 and 11).

Celebrate your body! Every part of it is a miracle. You were designed exactly as God intended. You have a vagina, uterus, ovaries, breasts, and everything else that's special about women, because God wanted it that way. He looked on Eve and declared her "very good." He feels the same way about you.

CHAPTER 6

# *The Changes Ahead for Boys*

**PUBERTY IS THE TIME** when a child's body is changing into an adult body. While girls go through puberty between ages nine and fifteen, and most at age eleven or twelve, most boys go through it between the ages of twelve and fifteen. Boys get a later start than girls. At the end of puberty a boy won't be fully grown, but *sexually* his body will function like a man's body.

Boys who go through puberty late sometimes are teased at school. If you know boys who are going through puberty late, you can help protect and support them as they go through this process. Being made fun of for something they can't control can hurt and discourage boys. You might ask your dad when he went through puberty, because you'll probably go through it around the same age he did.

## SIGNS OF THE TIMES

The first outward sign that a boy is beginning the process of puberty usually is the growth of pubic hair just above the penis. This hair often starts out fine and straight but becomes darker, thicker, and curlier. Most men also have some hair growing on their scrotums.

Soon after a boy begins to grow pubic hair, he'll probably have a general growth spurt. During the puberty period, the penis and scrotum have a growth spurt and change some in appearance. The skin on a boy's penis and scrotum looks a lot like the skin on the rest of his body, but as a boy becomes a man, this skin gets a bit darker and rougher than the rest of his skin.

## WISE ABOUT SIZE

As their penises and scrotums change, young men often worry whether their genitals are the "normal" size. When young men shower or change together in school, they may glance around to see how they compare with other boys. Remember that the size of your penis and scrotum changes depending on how you're feeling, what the temperature is, and so forth. If you're cold, your scrotum tucks up against your body and your penis shrinks to a smaller size. If you're warm and comfortable, your scrotum hangs loose and your penis is longer and a bit thicker.

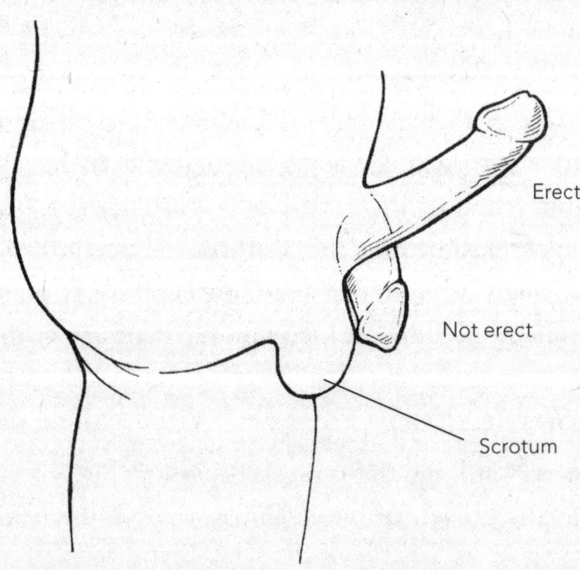

When a man becomes sexually excited (or aroused), his penis gets larger and harder, and it sticks out from his body instead of hanging loosely as it does most of the time. This is called having an *erection.*

Does the size of a young man's penis make any real difference? Are men's penises different sizes? While there are some minor differences in penis size, the differences are generally meaningless. In spite of what some boys whisper in jokes and locker-room bragging, the size of a man's penis has little or nothing to do with how much of a man he is. Nor does it affect how strong or brave he is or how much sexual joy, excitement, and pleasure he will have with his wife when he's married. A man's capacity to enjoy sex—and his capacity to help his wife enjoy sex—has very little to do with the size of his penis. It has much more to do with a husband and wife learning to express their love to each other. The size of your penis is nothing to worry about.

Another concern young men often have is about the way their scrotums look. It's normal for one of the testes inside the scrotum to hang a little lower and a little more in front than the other. Again, this is nothing to worry about. The size and shape of your penis and scrotum are just part of the way God has made you unique.

### HOW DO I LOOK?

During puberty, boys begin to get facial hair, starting with a few whiskers at the corners of their mouths (the beginnings of mustaches) or on the tips of their chins. Sideburns begin to thicken and grow down farther than they used to. Men's beards come in gradually, thick for some and sparse for others. During puberty, boys begin to get more hair in their armpits and on their arms, legs, and chests. But don't worry about how much or how little hair you have—a man's body hair has nothing to do with how much of a man he is or whether or not he'll be a good husband.

A young man's growth continues for some time after puberty. There are big differences in when men reach their full size. Some are at their full size by the time they are fifteen, but others continue growing into their early twenties. Before puberty, a boy can exercise all he wants and not develop big muscles. After puberty, young men who regularly exercise can become stronger and develop bigger muscles. Some men's bodies are built in such a way that exercise produces bigger muscles than those of other men who exercise just as much. This is just a difference between individuals.

## THE INSIDE STORY

We've been talking about the changes that are easy to see. But during puberty, changes happen on the inside as well.

It's the master gland at the bottom of the brain—the *pituitary gland*—that triggers a boy's body to begin the transformation into a man's body. The pituitary causes the boy's testes to begin making testosterone. Testosterone is the hormone that produces the growth of body hair and muscles, and it causes boys to increase in height and weight. But testosterone also brings about changes on the inside.

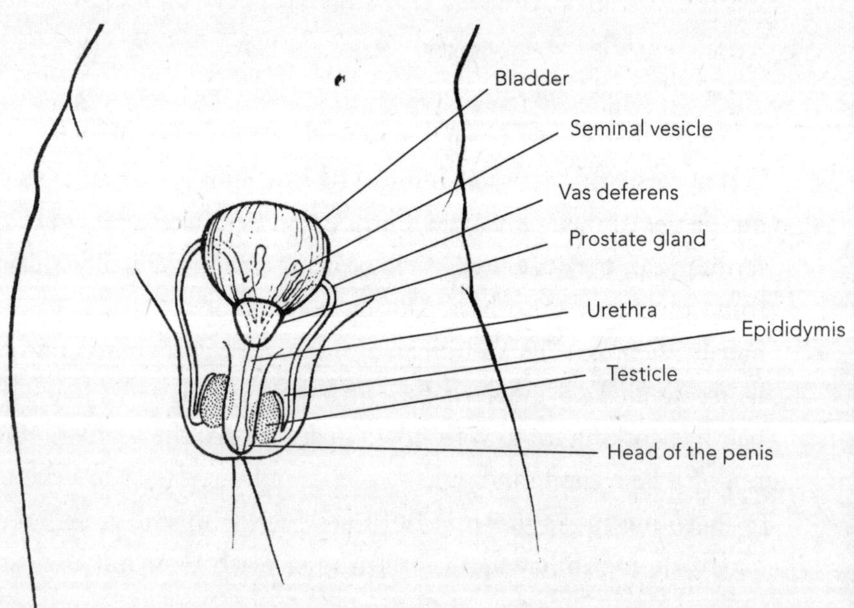

Your testes feel like hard balls, but each *testicle* (two testicles make the testes) is actually a densely packed group of tubes. On the inside of these tubes, sperm will be produced. In the spaces between the tubes, testosterone is produced and carried away by the blood vessels that nourish the testes. In each testicle the many tubes empty into an *epididymis*, a small holding structure where sperm come to full maturity and strength. A tiny tube called the *vas deferens* goes from the end of the epididymis inside your scrotal sack up inside your body. These two tubes—one from each testicle—go inside your body and around your *bladder* (the muscle bag that holds urine) and join together inside the prostate.

**The tubes** *in a man's testes are so tiny that if you were to uncoil the tubes in one testicle, they would stretch more than a quarter mile!*

The *urethra* is the tube that goes from the bottom of the bladder out to the tip of the penis. Under the bladder, wrapped around the urethra, is a gland called the *prostate*. It's inside the prostate that the two vas deferens tubes, one from each testicle, connect into the urethra.

### THE SPERM GAME

When the testes start producing adult-size doses of testosterone, they also begin producing sperm. The average man produces a hundred million sperm every twenty-four hours. To get an idea of that, imagine seventy thousand people sitting in a football stadium for a game. To produce a hundred million sperm in a day, a young man's testes must produce about as many sperm every minute as there are people in that football stadium!

Testosterone also starts the prostate and several other small, previously inactive glands working. These glands, which include a seminal vesicle on each side, begin to produce a fluid that's stored up in a man's body and mixes with the sperm coming out of his body when he has an ejaculation.

**WHAT'S ALL THE EXCITEMENT ABOUT?**

One of the biggest changes of puberty is that a young man begins to experience more sexual excitement or arousal, which usually causes more *erections*—when the penis gets harder and larger. Most boys have experienced erections (or in slang terms, "hard-ons") at different times in their lives—even baby boys get erections. Young men going through puberty get more and bigger erections.

The skin of the penis has lots of nerves in it, especially on the head or glans. God made these nerves in such a way that it feels good for the penis to be touched or rubbed. In this way, the head of the penis is just like a woman's clitoris: God designed it to experience pleasure. One of the changes of puberty is that the pleasure a young man feels from his penis increases. And when he feels pleasure from his penis, he may get an erection.

After a boy goes through puberty, he naturally becomes more interested in girls and thinks more frequently about sex. When he thought about sex before, he didn't have any particular reaction. But after puberty, when a young man thinks about sex, he often feels sexually aroused or excited, and he may begin to notice his penis becoming erect.

Men often have erections three or four times every night, during the periods of deepest sleep when they're also most likely to dream. In fact, it's common for men to wake up in the morning with erections. Having erections at these times doesn't appear to have anything to do with whether a man was dreaming at all or whether a dream was about sex in any way. Rather, there's something about the way a man's body deeply relaxes in these periods of sleep that's connected to having more blood flow to the penis.

Sometimes young men get erections for no obvious reasons. They don't remember thinking about sex or anything in particular, but they suddenly find themselves getting erections. This can happen, for example, when a young man is cooling down after exercising hard or playing a demanding sport. This is a normal part of growing up. It's very important for boys to realize that people generally can't tell that they have erections and it's nothing to worry about. But it can sometimes be a little embarrassing. It happens.

## HOW DOES AN ERECTION OCCUR?

The penis has skin on the outside. The urethra, the tube that passes urine, runs down its center. The rest of the penis inside the skin and around the urethra is made up of a spongy, soft tissue that's different from any other tissue in the body.

When a man feels pleasure from his penis being touched, his body responds to that pleasure by automatically sending more blood to the penis. This blood gets pressed into the spongy tissue of the penis so tightly that it makes the penis harder and bigger, sort of like filling up a water balloon. A balloon with no water in it is limp, but a balloon filled with water becomes harder, heavier, and stiffer. That's exactly what happens to a man's penis as it fills with blood. When it's not erect, a man's penis will usually be two or three inches long. When he gets an erection, his penis may be just more than twice that size, and it goes from loosely dangling downward to stiffly pointing out from his body.

Sometime during puberty a young man becomes able to have an *ejaculation*. From that time on, he's capable of becoming a father. He's certainly not ready to become a father or to have sex, but he's now producing sperm that can get a young woman pregnant. But what is an ejaculation?

We explain by using the example of a married couple. In this example, the husband begins to feel sexual excitement and have an erection when he's kissing and hugging his wife. If they then have sexual intercourse, the excitement and pleasure of the movement of his penis inside her vagina builds up until he feels a burst of intense pleasure. This burst of intense pleasure is called an *orgasm*. At the same time, a mixture of sperm and other fluids spurts out of his penis inside her vagina. That's an ejaculation.

How does it happen? The sperm produced by the man's testes mature and are stored in the epididymis just outside each testis. If the sperm aren't ejaculated out of his body in a few days, they die, are reabsorbed by the body, and are replaced by freshly made sperm. Moments before a man's orgasm, the man's sperm move quickly from the epididymides just outside the testes through the vas deferens tubes to the prostate. These tiny tubes are actually made of muscles that squeeze and release quickly all along their length, much the same way you squeeze toothpaste out of a tube.

In the prostate, the sperm mix with fluid from the prostate, the seminal vesicles, and other glands to make *semen*, the milky white fluid that's ejected out of the penis. These other fluids that make up the semen are designed to assist the sperm to live inside a woman's body so they can reach the egg to make a baby.

When a man ejaculates, the semen moves from the prostate through the urethra, which uses the same kind of muscular squeezing and releasing to push (ejaculate) the semen from the prostate out through the end of the penis. That is an ejaculation. The amount of fluid in an ejaculation is a small amount, about a teaspoon or two. Inside are 150 to 600 million sperm so tiny they can be seen only with a microscope.

**Semen:** *the milky white fluid that's a mixture of sperm and fluids from the prostate, seminal vesicles, and other glands. Semen spurts out of the penis when a man has an ejaculation.*

A man who has an orgasm begins to lose his erection soon after he ejaculates. This is a response built into men's bodies. For some time after a man has an orgasm, he cannot get another erection. For young men, this period when erection is impossible can be as short as a few minutes, but this period lengthens to a few hours for mature men and then to many hours or even a day for elderly men.

There are drugs that help men get erections faster and easier—you may see these advertised on TV. These are legitimate drugs, because there are medical conditions such as diabetes that interfere with nerve function and blood flow in the genitals, which makes it harder for those men to have erections.

### HOW CAN A DREAM BE WET?

Ejaculations do not happen only in marriage. Many boys experience their first ejaculations in their sleep. Doctors call this a *nocturnal* ("night") *emission*, but most people just call it a "wet dream." Wet dreams seem to occur naturally and are nothing to worry about or feel bad about. If you have one, you may have to change your underwear or wipe the semen off your sheets.

Sometimes during dreams, men will have orgasms with ejaculations. This can happen when they dream about sex. A young man may wake up after having a wet dream and realize he was dreaming about sex, about kissing a girlfriend, or simply about talking with a girl he really likes. Often, however, young men have wet dreams and can't remember their dreams having anything to do with sex. This, too, is perfectly normal and nothing to feel guilty about. People can't control what they dream. Some boys rarely experience wet dreams, and this is perfectly normal too.

### SUPER TRANSFORMER

Young men going through puberty are being transformed into adults. More changes lie ahead in how you feel, how you'll respond to women, and what's going to happen with your life. All of these changes are gifts from God. God wants you to use his gifts very carefully and bring him glory. He wants you to have the best life possible.

CHAPTER 7

# *How Does a Woman Become Pregnant?*

**BECOMING A PARENT** can be one of the most wonderful events in a person's life. The way a baby is conceived, develops inside its mother, and emerges into this world as a tiny, new person is truly miraculous. A birth is often a moment of spectacular joy for parents.

But pregnancy and childbirth aren't always wonderful. When a teenage girl gets pregnant outside of marriage, it changes the course of her whole life. An unmarried woman may suddenly find that the man who whispered, "I love you. I'll always be with you—I want to share my life with you," suddenly drops her when he finds out she's pregnant. Many men don't marry the women they get pregnant, and many also refuse to contribute any money or effort to care for these children, which leads to legal and emotional battles.

God made us so that the ideal context for children to grow into godly, strong adults is in families with loving mothers and fathers who are married and deeply committed to each other and to Jesus Christ. The combination of the love they provide together as parents and the special love mothers and fathers separately give to their children is the best formula for children to grow healthily. Scientific research has shown over and over that, on average, the best outcomes for children occur in such families.

How does someone become pregnant? Whether the pregnancy occurs in the right way (in the context of marriage) or in the wrong way (outside of marriage), the biological realities are amazing.

### NOW, *THAT'S* PLANNING AHEAD!

While a man produces millions of new sperm every day after puberty, a woman actually has all the eggs she'll ever have before she's even born. These eggs are preserved, nurtured, and kept safe in her ovaries through her childhood years. Each egg is tiny, smaller than the period at the end of this sentence. But this is gigantic compared to the size of the sperm produced by the man's body. When a girl starts puberty, she typically has several hundred thousand ova in her ovaries.

**Ovum:** *the word for one of the eggs in the woman's ovaries*

**Ova:** *the word for more than one egg in the woman's ovaries*

The sperm and the ova are like seeds, but there are some differences. Inside an apple seed is everything necessary for it to grow into an apple tree; all that is needed on the outside is water and nutrients. But neither a human sperm nor an ovum has everything needed to grow another human being. The chromosomes that contain our genes are critical for growing, and the sperm and the egg each have exactly half of the chromosomes needed to create a new human being. The chromosomes of the sperm have to join with the chromosomes of the egg in order to start a new human person.

This is why every human being is physically unique—one of a kind. A human being is formed from the chromosomes of a mother and the chromosomes of a father. Further, every sperm and every egg have slightly different samples of the father's and mother's genes. These unique chromosomes combine to make a new pattern that has never before been seen in the human race. There has never been anyone exactly like you, not even your brothers or sisters (unless you are an identical twin), and there will never again be anyone exactly like you.

**Genes:** *tiny strands of chemicals that direct from the inside of each cell the formation and activation of other cells during the development of a fetus and in the human body throughout its lifetime. The genes completely determine some human characteristics, such as eye or skin color. Genes have an influence—sometimes stronger and sometimes weaker—on other aspects of the body and personality, such as the tendency to gain weight or the tendency to have sharp eyesight.*

**Chromosomes:** *thousands of genes strung together in a group. The typical human cell contains all of its thousands of genes in twenty-three pairs of chromosomes.*

A man's body is always producing sperm; his body is always ready to help create a new baby. But a woman's body is only ready to create a baby at certain times each month. As a woman finishes a menstrual period, her body is getting ready for a possible pregnancy. Her hormones cause her ovaries to produce several mature ova (or eggs) and prepare them for release. Usually only one is released and able to be fertilized by joining with a sperm.

*The* **ovum** *and the* **sperm** *each contain half the chromosomes needed to make a whole and complete human being.*

About ten to twelve days after a woman has stopped her menstrual flow, her ovary releases the mature egg. The *fimbria*, the finger-like structures at the end of each fallopian tube, wave gently over the ovary inside the woman's abdomen, creating a movement that draws the egg into the tube. The egg travels down the fallopian tube. The trip is only a few inches, but it takes several days.

It's possible for a sperm to fertilize a newly released egg for about twenty-four hours. If a sperm doesn't meet and join with the egg during that time, the egg degenerates (dies) and passes out of the woman's body with her menstrual flow at the end of that cycle. She will not become pregnant that month.

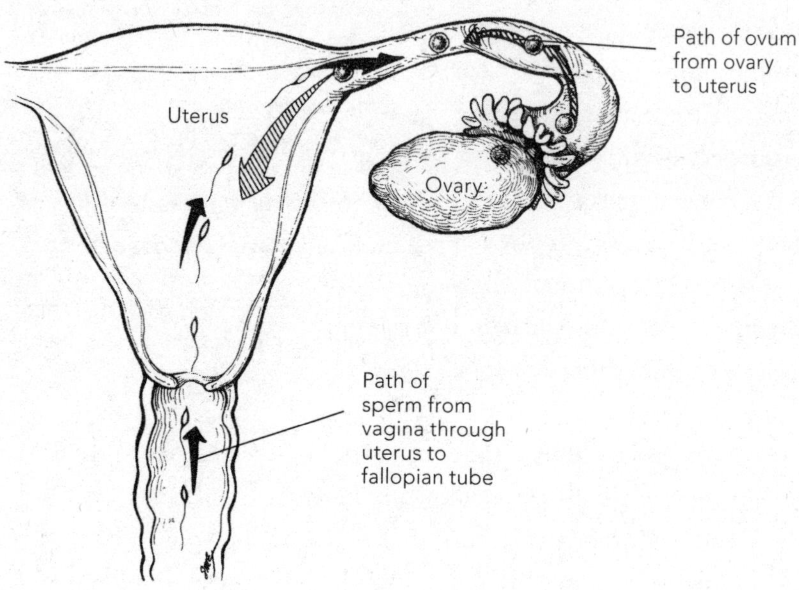


A woman can only get pregnant on that one day of each month when her ovum has been released and is alive, ready to meet a sperm. (We explain later why she does *not* have to have sex that day in order to get pregnant.) Some women can tell that they're ovulating because they feel wetness in their vaginas. This wetness comes from a woman's cervix (it's not the same as vaginal lubrication). Some women can feel slight twinges inside their abdomens when their ovaries release eggs. But most women don't know for sure each month when they can get pregnant. Certain women ovulate very early in their cycles—others ovulate late. There's really no time of the month when a person can be sure that ovulation hasn't occurred and pregnancy is impossible.

**Ovulation:** *the time when a woman's ovary releases a mature egg that can then join with a sperm*

## HOW DOES PREGNANCY HAPPEN?

When a man and a woman have sexual intercourse, the man's penis goes inside the woman's vagina, and when he ejaculates, between 150 and 600 million sperm are in the semen deposited in her vagina. Sperm are like tiny microscopic fish, with heads and tails that whip about to make them very efficient swimmers. Soon after they are out of the penis, they begin swimming.

Sperm are so tiny that their journey is very long. For a pregnancy to occur, they must travel from the woman's vagina up through the cervix, the uterus, and most of the fallopian tube, where one of them may join with the ovum or egg. Few sperm make it all the way. Only a fraction of the millions of ejaculated sperm make it out of the vagina and into the uterus. Only a fraction of those make it through the uterus to the openings of the fallopian tubes, and then half go into the wrong fallopian tube. Only a small number—probably only fifty to two hundred—ever get close to the egg. You can see why so many sperm are needed.

But it takes only one sperm to *fertilize* an egg. The instant that sperm is received through the outer layer of the egg, it becomes impossible for any other sperm to get inside it. Doctors say that the egg has been fertilized when the one sperm has gone into it. This is a complex and mysterious event.

Scientists used to speak of the "sperm penetrating the egg," but we now know that the egg cannot be penetrated until it releases a special hormone that allows penetration. The egg participates in drawing in the sperm. Once the sperm is inside the egg, the sperm's head comes apart, releasing all of its chromosomes—the genetic material of the man—into the inside of the egg. These chromosomes from the man quickly join with the chromosomes of the woman. At this moment, a baby is conceived.

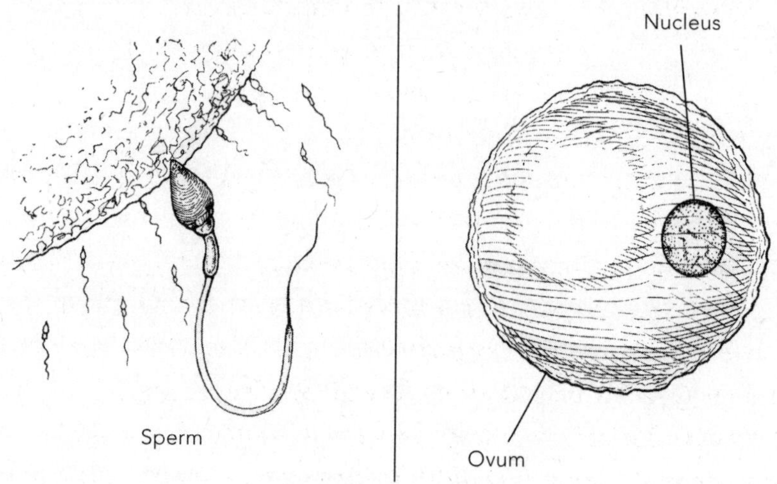


Sexual intercourse isn't the only way pregnancy can happen. You may have heard how some couples who have trouble getting pregnant will use *artificial insemination.* With artificial insemination, a woman doesn't get pregnant by having sexual intercourse—instead, a doctor places sperm inside her vagina or uterus through a plastic tube.

## IS GETTING PREGNANT HARD OR EASY?

Women don't get pregnant every time they have sexual intercourse. The egg can be fertilized only for about twenty-four hours before it begins to break apart and die. Sperm, though, live between one and three days or even up to five days. This usually means there are about three or four days each month when sexual intercourse can lead to a woman getting pregnant.

If she has sexual intercourse two or three days *before* she ovulates, her husband's sperm may be in the fallopian tubes and still alive right when the egg is released. This egg might get fertilized early in its journey down the fallopian tubes. On the other hand, if the husband and wife have sexual intercourse just as the egg is released, the egg may stay alive just long enough for the fastest sperm to reach it.

Sometimes, for reasons we don't understand, the sperm simply fail to reach the ovum. And sometimes, even though they reach the ovum, fertilization does not take place; either the sperm can't get inside the egg or they just miss it.

It may be hard for some women to get pregnant. Many things can go wrong. Some couples who really want babies can find that they have trouble getting pregnant. But it's much easier for most young women to get pregnant than many of us realize. Just under one million teenage women get pregnant every year, and most of them didn't mean to. Most women don't know with certainty when they ovulate, and we don't ever know exactly how long the man's sperm might live. Some people try to prevent pregnancy by guessing when the woman is going to ovulate, but those guesses are often wrong.

Some people try to prevent pregnancy in ways that are quite ridiculous. For example, if a woman gets up immediately after having sex and jumps up and down, she won't be able to "shake the sperm out of her vagina." Sperm immediately begin swimming when they get inside the vagina, and even if a woman jumps up and down, enough sperm will stay inside her that she could become pregnant. Some people think that stopping sexual intercourse before the man has an ejaculation is safe. Wrong! There's often a tiny drop of fluid that comes from a man's penis even before he ejaculates, and this tiny drop sometimes contains live sperm. It takes only one sperm to get a woman pregnant.

## HOW DO TWINS HAPPEN?

Any birth of more than one baby is called a *multiple birth.* Multiple births include twins (two babies), triplets (three), quadruplets (four), and so forth. There are two types of multiple births. One happens when only one egg is released and gets fertilized. The other occurs when the woman releases more than one egg and more than one get fertilized.

**Multiple births:** *when a woman gives birth to more than one child from a single pregnancy*

*Identical twins* start off the same way all single births do, with the woman releasing one egg that's fertilized by one sperm. But very early on in the pregnancy, the fertilized egg splits in two and begins to develop as two babies rather than one. These two babies have the exact same chromosomes. Because it's the chromosomes that cause us to have certain physical and psychological characteristics, these twins will look just alike and often have similar personalities. Remember earlier when we said that every human being is different except identical twins. Identical twins are genetically the same. They do become different, however, because they are distinct persons in God's eyes and they have unique experiences.

If the woman releases two (or even three or four) eggs, and if each joins with a different sperm, the woman will have twins (or triplets or quadruplets) that are not identical—these are called *fraternal twins.* Because each fraternal twin comes from a different egg and a different sperm, they usually look no more alike than do other brothers and sisters in the family. They have no reason to look identical, as their chromosomes are just as different as those of a brother and sister born five years apart.

Nothing can be done to cause a woman to have identical twins, and no one is sure why it happens. Fraternal pregnancies appear to happen because some women's bodies just release more than one egg. Also, some drugs that doctors can give women who have trouble getting pregnant cause the women's ovaries to release multiple eggs. Women on these drugs are more likely than other women to have multiple births. Births of four babies or more rarely happen without use of these drugs.

## THE REST OF THE STORY

Once the man's sperm fertilizes the woman's egg, a new life is formed.[1] As complex as this has been, even more adventures await the developing child. We continue the rest of the story in the next chapter.

CHAPTER 8

# *How Does the Baby Develop and the Mother Give Birth?*

**AFTER AN EGG** is fertilized, a new human life has begun. How can it survive inside the mother's body? God's design truly is miraculous.

The fertilized egg continues down the fallopian tube for about a week until it comes into the uterus. At first it's only one cell with unique chromosomes that are a mixture of genes from the woman and man. Even as it journeys down the fallopian tube, it begins to divide. One cell splits into two, two into four, and on and on. The dividing starts slowly but soon picks up speed. This begins the remarkable growth of the baby. At first the cells divide without growing, and within a day or two, they become a compact ball of cells the same size as the original egg.

The next critical stage is for the developing baby to attach to the side of the uterus. This is called *implantation*. If the tiny ball of cells implants, it's likely to grow and be born a healthy, whole baby. If it doesn't implant and continues down the uterus and through the cervix, it will die from lack of nutrition and be passed out of the woman's body. Usually when this happens, the woman never knows that her egg was fertilized and a new life conceived. No one knows why some babies implant and others do not.

If the baby implants, it continues to develop. With nourishment it receives from the uterine wall, it begins to grow rapidly while its cells continue to divide and multiply at extraordinary speed. At first the dividing cells all look the same, but soon different cells form different kinds of tissue that come together to form different organs that perform specific jobs. The genes direct this specialization.

At the time of this early growth, some of the cells form a *placenta* right where the baby connects to the wall of the uterus. The placenta is an organ full of blood vessels that take oxygen and food from the blood of the mother through the wall of her uterus and pass them into the blood of the baby. From the placenta, the *umbilical cord* carries these nutrients into the baby's body. The umbilical cord connects to the baby's body at its navel, or belly button.

God designed the mother's body not only to feed the developing baby but to protect it as well. The *amniotic sac* filled with *amniotic fluid* forms around the baby inside the uterus. The amniotic fluid and sac form a sort of cushion so that even if the pregnant woman runs or jumps up and down, the baby is largely undisturbed as it floats in its protective sac. The developing baby lives in this fluid for its entire nine-month prenatal (or pre-birth) life quite comfortably because its oxygen supply comes from the mother through the umbilical cord rather than through normal breathing. For extra protection, a soft plug forms in the center opening of the cervix, effectively sealing off the baby from the outside world and making the baby completely dependent on its mother during the entire pregnancy.

Vital organs begin to form quickly. A tiny brain forms, followed by a tiny spinal cord. The heart, lungs, liver, and other internal organs start to form. Arm buds, leg buds, and a tail form. The tail disappears later, while the arms and legs lengthen as the baby's other parts grow and develop rapidly.

*Your* **navel** *is the scar that was left when your umbilical cord dried up and fell off after you were born.*

The baby develops at incredible speed. If we grew as fast after we were born as we did while we were in our mothers' uteruses, we would be the size of elephants by the time we were four or five years old. Within the span of nine months, a baby grows from one cell tinier than a grain of sand to an average of seven or eight pounds and about twenty-one inches long. *That's* astounding growth!

For reasons not well understood, some babies die after they begin to grow in their mothers' uteruses. This is called *miscarriage.* Research suggests that babies who die before they're born often have something seriously wrong with their bodies, something that would make it impossible for them to live. But no one knows why most miscarriages occur.

### HOW DOES A WOMAN KNOW SHE'S PREGNANT?

One of the first signs that a woman is pregnant is that she doesn't have her next menstrual period when she expects it. The purpose of the menstrual cycle is for the woman's uterus to get ready to become pregnant. Once she's pregnant, the developing baby needs the extra blood from the mother to give it oxygen and food. While women are pregnant, they normally don't have any bleeding or menstrual flow.

Just because a woman misses her period doesn't mean she's pregnant. There are various reasons a woman might not have her menstrual flow at the normal time, such as having been sick, very upset, or overly tired.

Sometime during the two weeks after a woman has missed her period, some unique chemicals appear in her urine and blood that, when tested, show whether or not she's pregnant. About the same time, if a woman is pregnant, she may begin to experience signs such as mild nausea. Because most pregnant women have this sick-to-their-stomachs feeling more frequently in the morning, it's called morning sickness. This nausea usually stops after several weeks.

## IS THERE ENOUGH ROOM?

How does a pregnant woman's body make room for a baby? Her uterus, which is normally the size of her closed fist, grows large enough to hold even a ten- or eleven-pound baby. To make room for this baby, her belly stretches outward and her other internal organs get pressed and pushed out of the way. For example, toward the end of their pregnancies, most women find they have to go to the bathroom much more often because their bladders are compressed and not able to hold as much urine. Many pregnant women eat several small meals daily instead of three regular meals because their stomachs and intestines can't hold as much food as they usually do.

Pregnant women often experience muscle aches because their bodies aren't used to carrying the extra weight that comes with pregnancy. Most women gain a total of twenty-five to thirty-five pounds during their pregnancies (including the weight of the baby, which averages between seven and eight pounds). Mothers gain additional weight beyond the weight of their babies because of other changes in their bodies, such as in their breasts. Women's breasts usually grow in size as the milk ducts expand and get ready for milk production. That milk production is called *lactation*.

## IT SOUNDS LIKE A LOT OF WORK

The woman's body begins the process of the birth of the baby after about nine months. Sometimes the first sign of the beginning of the birth process is a sudden release through the woman's vagina of the plug in the cervix; this is sometimes called a "bloody show" because the plug is partially made up of dead or dying blood cells. Or the first sign could be the sudden release of the amniotic fluid; women describe this as their "water breaking."

But the most common first sign of the birth process beginning is the experience of strong contractions of the uterus that we call labor pains. In each of these contractions, which start out milder and spaced further apart, the sheets of muscle making up the uterus squeeze and force the baby down lower. The strongest muscles in the uterus are at the top—they begin to contract to push the baby out through the cervix and vagina.

**Labor:** *the hard work of giving birth to a baby*

For the average woman, labor lasts about fourteen hours for the first child and is shorter for subsequent children. During those hours, the cervix, which is normally closed, slowly opens. Women's hips are able to stretch and flex so the baby can go through the circle of bone at the base of the hips, through the cervix, and out of the vagina. If the entire birth process takes fourteen hours, the first thirteen may be required just to get the hips and cervix to open large enough for the baby's head to come through. Once they're open enough, the birth proceeds very rapidly.

The woman begins to push hard as she experiences her intense labor contractions to get the baby through the cervix and the vagina. The vagina is normally a small tube, but it stretches during the birth process to let the baby come through. The normal way of delivery is for the baby to come out headfirst. As the woman pushes, the baby's head, which is specially designed to help the cervix open and pass through the vagina, appears in the outside world for the first time. As the woman continues to push, the rest of the baby's body comes out. In order to disconnect the baby from the placenta, the doctor, midwife, or dad cuts the umbilical cord after the baby is out. Within minutes after the baby comes out of the woman's vagina, the rest of the umbilical cord and the placenta come out as well.

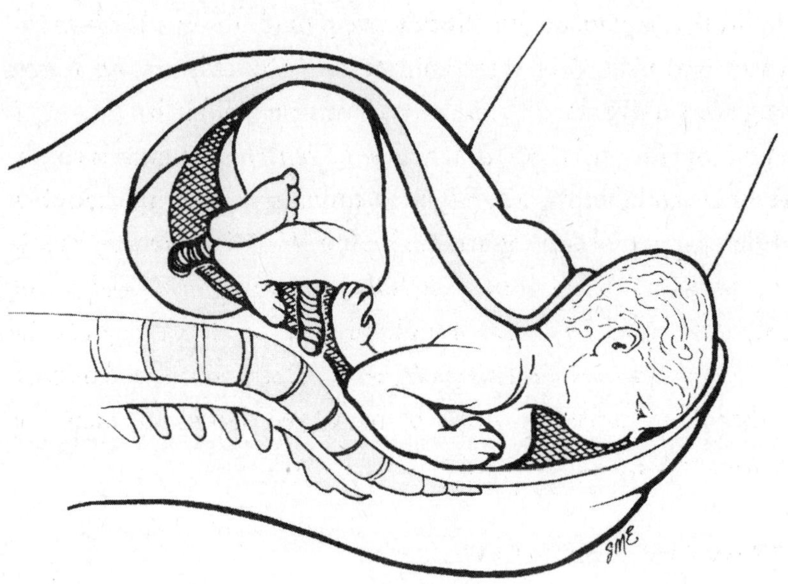

**OUCH!**

Childbirth hurts. But a woman's body is very resilient, designed by God for this purpose. After giving birth to a child, a woman is extremely tired and overwhelmed with how much pain and work it was, but she also is overjoyed with the marvelous gift of her baby. She usually is able to hold it and be with it right away.

It takes a number of months for a woman's body to return completely to normal. The uterus, which was so stretched out of shape, slowly returns to its original size. The woman usually loses much of the extra weight she gained. Her hips return to their firm condition, and her vagina and cervix heal from the stretching.

Not all babies can be born through their mothers' vaginas. Sometimes if a baby isn't in the head-down position, a doctor might decide it's too big of a risk for the mother to give birth through her vagina, so the doctor will deliver the baby through an operation. A doctor will also sometimes deliver a baby this way when the passageway through a woman's hips is not big enough to let a big baby be born or when the doctor is afraid that a baby may not be strong enough to survive the difficult process of a vaginal birth.

This operation is called a *caesarean section*. Doctors give the mother an anesthetic that makes her numb to pain, and then they make a cut right above the woman's pubic hair through the muscle to the woman's uterus. They carefully cut through the wall of the uterus and remove the baby through this incision. Then they sew the wall of the uterus, the muscles of the abdomen, and the skin back together. The woman has a healthy baby even though the baby was not delivered through the vagina.

## GETTING THE RIGHT START

Just as God made women's bodies to care for babies before birth, he made women's breasts to feed their babies after they're born. During the first few days after a baby's birth, its mother's breasts make a substance called *colostrum*. Colostrum has some food value, but this watery, yellow liquid mainly acts as medicine for the baby, helping it resist diseases and infections that might threaten its life in its first few weeks in the world.

Within several days, the mother's milk begins to be produced; this is called *lactation*. The milk that is made in a human mother's breasts is the perfect food for babies. Babies would be malnourished and grow up abnormal if they were fed nothing but cow's milk.

When a woman is lactating, she eats more than she normally would because her body requires extra food to make milk. The milk builds up in her breasts over two to three hours. When the baby begins to suckle on her breast, milk is released from the milk glands to flow out of her nipple. For many different reasons, some women choose to feed their babies specially designed baby formula rather than nurse them with their own breast milk.

Most babies live on nothing but their mothers' milk (or formula from a bottle) for five to eight months before parents begin to give them other kinds of simple foods they can digest. Some babies will stop nursing soon after they begin to eat solid foods, while others continue to nurse—though much less than they used to—for months and even years after they begin to eat solids.

### A TRUE MIRACLE!

What a miracle that any of us are born! What a gift God gave us in our sexuality—the gift of marriage and sexual intercourse and the ability to have children. What does God say about how we should handle this beautiful gift? That's our next subject.

PART 3

# *Putting It into Practice: The Hard Questions*

CHAPTER 9

# *False Advertising: A Failed Revolution*

**HAVE YOU EVER FELT CHEATED**? Watched a trailer for what looked like a spectacular movie, only to find the movie a dud? Paid for an exciting video game that ended up being boring or a new piece of technology that didn't work? Had a friend promise to be there for you and then leave you hanging?

It's frustrating to feel cheated. Nobody likes it.

As you move into your teenage years, you'll have to make decisions about what you believe about sex. What it is for, when to do it, who to do it with, and on and on. Millions of people have believed the false promises of the sexual revolution that began decades ago, and those false promises are being sold with louder voices and more pressure today than perhaps ever before.

Each one of us is in the same basic situation every day, even right now, that Adam and Eve were in the Garden of Eden. God is lovingly calling us to follow him into a life of rich, pure, beautiful possibilities, while the evil one twists God's words to lure us down paths that lead to brokenness, pain, disappointment, and distress. This chapter attempts to shine a light on the real decisions you have ahead and where they lead.

In the first chapter of this book, we presented four teens who thought about the world and about sex in very different ways: the bold materialist, the inward seeker, the relaxed churchgoer, and the Jesus-follower. The belief of the Jesus-follower is that full sexual intimacy is meant *only* as a special act to bond one wife and one husband who are united for life and are open to the gift of children. This is why sex should be reserved for marriage. The other three positions were more blasé, saying things like "Enjoy without limits!" or "There are no hard rules—it all depends." Where did these views come from?

## THE REVOLUTION THAT SUCCEEDED

Until fairly recently, most people believed there was something special about sex that made it worth reserving for marriage. This was what the Christian church taught across the world (as did Judaism, Islam, and other religions too). Many nonbelievers accepted this same assumption that sex was to be reserved for marriage. There were people who broke the rules, but most people—even the rule breakers—thought there was something wrong or risky about their actions. Things have changed.

This may seem like ancient history now, but sixty or seventy years ago, a "sexual revolution" began that changed people's perceptions of sex. Revolutions happen for a reason. One important factor in this sexual revolution was science. Medical advances gave us more effective treatments for sexually transmitted infections and more effective birth control methods (ways to prevent pregnancy). Together, these developments made sex outside of marriage seem less risky.

More importantly, this was a time of great cynicism and pessimism.

For several centuries, Western society had been promoting the idea that as we learned more through human reason, everything was getting better. Many believed that we were on an inevitable path of progress that would make people happier, more fulfilled, and more prosperous.

But after multiple wars in the 1900s in which millions died and in the face of broken political promises, ethical scandals, failed agreements, and more and more evidence that progress was the result of random chance or was a lie, a new seductive mind-set came along: "Look inside; trust your feelings. You are your own ultimate authority."

It sounds simple, doesn't it? But this simple message had profound implications. It taught people that institutions aren't to be trusted—not governments, not schools, not corporations and companies, and *especially* not churches or religions.

The new movement asked, "Who are you? How should you behave?" And it answered, "Don't expect others to answer the question. *You* are the answer. You have the answer inside you. If you conform to what institutions tell you, you're letting yourself be a slave to them. Don't be a slave—be a master. Chart your own destiny."

When it came to sex, the message was "Enjoy and experiment—the more the better. Be genuine to yourself, follow your feelings, and all will be well."

In responding to this shift of views, the Christian church failed in two big ways. First, in response to those who said that sex is great and we should all just enjoy it, many representatives of the church responded with negative cries of "Shame on you! Sex outside of marriage is bad, bad, *bad*!" Christians came across as rigid and fearful; they were negative and had nothing positive to offer.

Even worse, though, were the actions of some church authorities and religious leaders who committed adultery, indulged in gay sex on the side, and even sexually abused children. Such failures gave many reason to disregard the church or "organized religion" as having any integrity or authority. Even worse, these leaders' actions cast a shadow on Jesus Christ himself since they claimed to represent him.

Before we go any further, we have to emphasize that these failures of the Christian church were sins. The church did a lot of shaming and preached a lot of rigid rules, and some church leaders committed sexual sins and abuses. Guilty as charged. This cannot be explained away.

But while it cannot be explained away, it can be explained. The church isn't a sanctuary of the perfect—it's a hospital for the sick and broken, including some people who are so broken that they inflict their pain on others. And sadly, as Scripture warns us, wolves intent on doing evil sometimes hide among the sheep (God's true children; see Matthew 7:15; Acts 20:29-30). Our hope is not in the church or in the pastor—our hope is in Jesus Christ, who died on the cross for us, defeated death to live again, and will vanquish all brokenness and sickness. He alone is the source of all forgiveness and healing. May Christ forgive those church leaders who had nothing to say except "Shame!" May Christ forgive those whose hypocritical, sinful behavior caused others to doubt the message and person of Jesus.

In part, this book and the others in the God's Design for Sex series are an attempt to make up for those church failings. While naming and begging forgiveness for the ways that God's people have failed to represent Christ well, we want to emphasize that sex and our sexuality are an amazingly good gift and blessing. The boundaries God has put in place for us both protect us from evil and help bring goodness and joy.

## THE PROMISES OF THE REVOLUTION

This sexual revolution has largely succeeded in replacing the old views about saving sex for marriage—those attitudes are now held by a clear minority. "Throw out the bad guys, and overturn the old ways of thinking," the majority says. "We'll make it better. And sex? Enjoy it as you see fit: for some, the more the better, and for others, do as your conscience dictates. Be genuine to yourself, and follow your feelings, including—even especially including—your sexual feelings."

Revolutionaries make promises. What were the promises of the sexual revolution? Simply put, "Follow us and our plan, and life in general, relationships, and sex will all get better."

If the revolution has worked, the following outcomes should be evident by now: On average, people should be

- having more sex,
- happier in their intimate relationships (regardless of whether they're married or not) and better connected to family and friends,
- happier overall, and
- doing so well that their children are flourishing as a result.

So how's this revolution working out?

## THE REVOLUTION THAT'S FAILING

Things do not seem to be working out so well. Here's a summary of findings from several respected scientists whose conclusions are generally (but not universally) accepted:

*Are adults having more sex?* No.

With the growing acceptance of the beliefs of the sexual revolution, adults are actually having less sex, not more. In the United States, scientists have found that the average percentage of adults having sexual intercourse "at least once a week dropped from 45% in 1996 to 22% in 2016."[1] Similarly, in Britain in 1990, both women and men who were sexually active reported having sexual intercourse five times per month, but in 2000, the average had fallen to four times per month, and in 2010 it had fallen to three times per month.[2] Similar findings have emerged wherever the beliefs of the sexual revolution have taken firm root.

This decline in the frequency of sex may have many causes. One may be a declining percentage of the groups most likely to have sex, namely those who are married or cohabiting (living together without being married).[3] The prominence of pornography may also play a role; so also may our growing reliance on "social media" that too often make us less social and more isolated. Whatever the cause, people are having less sex, not more.

*Are adults happier in their intimate relationships and better connected to family and friends?* No.

The statistics throughout North America and Europe are clear: The percentage of people who marry is going down, and for those who marry, the average age continues to go up. Reporting recently that a "record share of Americans have never married," an important study on marriage found that in the early 1960s, only 28 percent of men and 13 percent of women age twenty-five or younger had never married. By 2012, 78 percent of men and 67 percent of women had never married, a huge shift. It also reported that "the median age at first marriage is now 27 for women and 29 for men, up from 20 for women and 23 for men in 1960."[4]

*Cohabitation*—living together without being married—is increasingly taking the place of marriage, which is bad news for kids mainly because it tends to be a less stable family structure, which increases a number of other risks for children, as we will discuss in a bit.

With marriage in decline and cohabitation often failing as a substitute, we are not surprised to find that people today feel more loneliness, not less. From the 1980s to 2017, the rate of loneliness has doubled from 20 percent to 40 percent.[5] What explains this?

Harvard scientist Robert Putnam said this happens because people today increasingly live alone and socialize less with family, friends, and community groups such as churches or clubs.[6] But why would that be the case? Sociologist Eric Klinenberg argued that this destructive individualism is based on our new "most sacred modern values [of] freedom, autonomy, control of one's time and space, and the search for individual fulfillment,"[7] the same basic values promoted by the sexual revolution. Maybe, Putnam conjectured, such highest values result in patterns of life that create loneliness.

*Are adults happier overall?* No.

Over the past fifty years, surveys have asked thousands of US and European adults about overall happiness and have documented a long slide downward.[8] The suicide rate is at epidemic proportions for all age groups except the elderly. Loneliness, isolation from friends and family, loss of meaning, and hopelessness all contribute to people choosing to commit suicide. People who have active religious faith have more of a sense of meaning and hope and are thus less at risk of suicide, and religious faith and practice have been on the decline.[9]

*Are children flourishing today due to the sexual revolution?* No.

Some of you reading this book may have a single mom or single dad, be adopted, or live with a grandparent or foster parent. Please do not take the following as criticism of you or your family. And don't read it as a prediction that your life is going to have negative outcomes. A lot of kids from such families flourish thanks to their own determination and the excellent support they get from their families.

But the evidence is clear. Children are most likely to thrive in stable homes where two parents—a mom and dad—work together to meet the needs of the kids. On average, children from a traditional two-parent, married family do better on almost every important measurable variable compared to children living in alternative circumstances.[10] Cohabitation, for example, "is associated with several factors that have the potential to reduce children's wellbeing, including lower levels of parental education and fewer legal protections. Most importantly, cohabitation is often a marker of family instability, which is strongly associated with poorer outcomes for children."[11]

Because marriage is less likely than average among those who are poorer and less educated, the children in these families have fewer resources. Their single parents scramble to balance work and parenting, and the families have less money and fewer educational resources.

In the words of the experts who issued a joint report from a top-tier university and think tank, "Most scholars now agree that children raised by two biological parents in a stable marriage do better than children in other family forms across a wide range of outcomes."[12] The "outcomes" they refer to include many variables, such as the likelihood these children will get good grades in school, graduate from high school and go to college, not use drugs, not drink excessively, not engage or experiment with risky sex, not experience emotional or mental problems, and not get arrested.

If you're a child from a single-parent or other nontraditional family, don't be discouraged. Talk with your parent, a youth leader or minister, or a trusted school counselor or teacher (or all of them) to get the resources you need to become the person God is calling you to be. Making good choices will be critical in determining what kind of adult you will eventually become.

### "YOU WILL RECOGNIZE THEM BY THEIR FRUITS" (MATTHEW 7:16)

Fewer and fewer people share the Christian belief that sex should be reserved for a lifetime marriage union of a man and woman. The mind-set of the sexual revolution is now deeply ingrained in our culture. It shapes what you hear about sex in popular music, see on television, read in books, hear about in sex education classes, see in movies, and overhear in the chatter at school.

But has the sexual revolution been good for people? There's good evidence that the answer is no. On average, people

- are having less sex,
- are less likely to get married and have children,
- are less happy and are more lonely and isolated, and
- are seeing that those children being raised without the blessing of two parents are bearing some of the bad consequences.

Jesus told us that we can recognize true believers by the good fruit in their lives. The same can be said about belief systems: We can partly judge them by their results. By this standard, the mind-set of the sexual revolution looks questionable. We hope that this encourages you to think seriously about the decisions that lie ahead for you.

In the next chapter, we apply similar thinking. If the Christian vision for sexuality is true, we might expect things to go better when we live by those guidelines. Let's look at those issues next.

## CHAPTER 10

# *Saving Sex for Marriage: Thinking Practically*

**SOMETIMES IT SEEMS** as if everyone is having sex. Some kids in high school talk as if they have sex all the time. Characters on television and in movies often move quickly from their first meetings to bedroom scenes. In many school sex-education classes, there's enthusiasm about using birth control when you do have sex but only joking and cynicism about choosing not to have sex. Many people today use the word *virgin* (anybody who has not yet had sexual intercourse) as an insult instead of a compliment (as it is in the Bible). A teenager who chooses not to have sex can feel a little lonely.

People will try to convince you that saving sexual intercourse for marriage is stupid. They will tell you things like the following:

- "Sex is the very best way to express affection and love. If you really love someone, you'll have sex."

- "You must have sex to be a normal, mature, grown-up person."
- "The desire for sex is so strong it cannot be resisted."
- "It's important to try sex before you get married to make sure you're sexually compatible."
- "It's important to have sex to practice for marriage."
- "Sex is always good."

Every one of these arguments is wrong. In the next chapter we talk about how these arguments are misguided because they misrepresent what sex is for and what sex means to God. In this chapter, we talk about how these arguments fail to take into account the physical risks of having sex outside of marriage.

### SOME STRAIGHT TALK ABOUT SAFE SEX

You've probably heard about the importance of "safe sex." Seeking safety is reasonable, because sex can be dangerous to one or both partners. There are two main physical dangers of sex outside of marriage.

The first is the serious risk of sexually transmitted infections or sexually transmitted diseases (STIs or STDs—different terms for the same thing). Here's a brief look at some of the most common STIs:

**Sexually transmitted infections**, *or* **STIs**, *are spread by people having sex. The germs causing these infections are either concentrated in a man's semen and a woman's vaginal lubrication or are on or in the delicate tissues of the man's and woman's genitals.*

*Chlamydia* is a bacterial infection spread by sex. If detected early, it can be treated effectively. It often goes undetected, however, because chlamydia has no noticeable symptoms. Infected people rarely think they have a disease and so never get diagnosed and treated. However, its effects on women can be profound. While it goes undetected, the chlamydia infection spreads, causing scar tissue in a woman's uterus and fallopian tubes. If untreated, it often leaves the infected woman unable to have children.

*HPV (human papillomavirus)* is a viral infection estimated to be the most common and rapidly spreading STI. At this time, there are no known cures for HPV. Like chlamydia, it usually has no noticeable symptoms (except those varieties that cause warts on your genitals and elsewhere). People with HPV are often completely unaware of it. Women who get HPV are at great risk for developing cancer of the cervix later in life, which is a very dangerous cancer.

*Trichomoniasis* is an infection from a type of protozoa, a single-celled parasite that flourishes in the urinary tract of a man and in the vagina and urinary tract of a woman. Men rarely have any symptoms of infection, and some women have no symptoms. People who have trichomoniasis are more vulnerable to being infected with HIV (human immunodeficiency virus), and women who have it are more likely to deliver premature babies if they get pregnant.

The highly contagious nature and lack of symptoms of these three diseases explains why they're the most common STIs. Infected carriers often go on having sex, infecting other people. These diseases are at near epidemic levels among young adults, especially college students. Some estimates are that between 30 and 50 percent of female college students have one or more of these STIs. These women unknowingly face real and potentially tragic consequences from these infections.

The most deadly STI is *HIV*, the infection that results in *AIDS* (acquired immunodeficiency syndrome). HIV gets into the cells of a person's body and begins to kill the specialized immune cells made to fight other diseases.

If untreated, an HIV-infected person becomes less and less capable of fighting off other diseases and eventually dies from one of these other diseases. This state of having a weak immune system and many other infections is called AIDS. People don't really die of HIV—they die from other diseases that their bodies could have protected them from if HIV had not wrecked their abilities to fight off those diseases.

**STIs** *are more common today than at any other time in history. Several studies have shown that more than one-third of all college women have already had at least one STI by the time they're twenty-one years old.*

HIV/AIDS is a terrible disease. In the 1980s and '90s, almost everyone who got HIV died of AIDS within a few years. Today, new drugs help people with HIV (or "HIV-positive" people) live much longer. Some people have lived twenty years or more with the disease and may live a normal life span. They're never cured of HIV; they will get sick if they stop taking medicine, but with the proper medication they can live fairly normal lives. Unfortunately, they can still infect other people. Estimates are that more than forty million people have died of AIDS since the disease first appeared in Africa, and about forty million more people currently have and live with HIV. Most of the infected are in Africa, but more than one million of them are in the United States.

**HIV:** *human immunodeficiency virus*

**AIDS:** *acquired immunodeficiency syndrome*

The HIV virus is especially concentrated in blood, semen, and vaginal lubrication. Thus, most people who have HIV got it from having sex with someone who had it. But not everyone gets HIV this way.

Some people get it when they take drugs using a needle that has HIV on it. Some children are infected by their HIV-positive mothers, who passed it to their babies through their blood during pregnancy or after birth through their breast milk. A few others became infected through blood transfusions before doctors knew how to make sure blood was clean from HIV.

We urge you to look further into other common STIs, including genital herpes, gonorrhea, syphilis, viral hepatitis, and others. These are ugly diseases, all of which are passed by infected people to their sexual partners. This is why people say that *when you have sex with someone, you're having sex with every other person your partner ever had sex with*.

Let's say a sixteen-year-old girl who has never had sex before feels that she's in love and chooses to have sex with her eighteen-year-old boyfriend. Is she safe because she's never had sex before? If her boyfriend has had sex with three other women before her and one of those other women had sex with six different men, then diseases from any of those nine different people could infect her. This is the way sexually transmitted diseases are passed.

*How can you be sure you never get one of these sexually transmitted diseases?* Simple. If you save sexual intercourse and all sexual intimacy (in chapter 12 we talk about what this means) for the person you marry, and if that person also saves sex for marriage with you, then neither of you ever has to worry about having a sexually transmitted disease.

## AND THEN THERE'S PREGNANCY . . .

The second main physical danger of sexual intercourse is for the woman to get pregnant. Young women risk serious medical problems from getting pregnant as teenagers. Babies born to teenage mothers are more likely to be born underweight or premature. Teenage mothers are more likely to have various medical problems as a result of pregnancy and childbirth.

There are other concerns as well. The basic options for a pregnant young woman are to abort the baby, have the baby and place it for adoption, or keep and raise the baby. A young woman who chooses to have an abortion will have to go through life knowing she let a doctor kill her baby because she didn't want it. Placing a baby for adoption is a wonderful gift to the adoptive parents and to the baby who will be raised by parents ready for parenthood. But it changes a young woman's life to go through the pregnancy, and placing a baby for adoption is a hard experience that raises many conflicted feelings of guilt and grief.

If the young woman chooses to have and keep the baby, her friendships may change. Some friends may pull away from her because they can't relate to what she's going through. Teenage mothers are more likely to drop out of school and to live in poverty because they can't get jobs. Teenage fathers are less likely to support the mothers of their children with money or help than are married fathers. Children who grow up with only one parent do not do as well in school, they get into trouble with the police more often, and they're more likely to have children of their own while they are still teenagers than are children whose parents are married. There are big risks when young unmarried women get pregnant.

## PROTECTING AGAINST TROUBLE

What about birth control or contraceptives? How effective are the medications or methods that protect and defend against STIs and pregnancy? Let's look at the two most common methods: the birth control pill and the condom.

Birth control pills contain artificial versions of female hormones that do two things: (1) They suppress or delay ovulation (the release of the egg that might otherwise be fertilized), and (2) they make the woman's uterus less able to receive a growing, fertilized egg.

Taken with absolute consistency, birth control pills drastically reduce the chances of a woman becoming pregnant when she has sex. Pay attention, however, to the fact that we said they reduce rather than eliminate the chances. The pill is not foolproof, even when taken regularly.

Two other things: First, research shows that teenage women find it difficult to take the pill in the disciplined way necessary for it to be effective. With the distractions and challenges of adolescent years, teenagers on the pill are more likely than adult women to get pregnant anyway.

Second, many people falsely believe that a pill that protects against pregnancy somehow also protects against STIs. Sadly, it does not. For that protection, there is the condom.

A condom is shaped like a balloon; most are made of latex, the same material doctors' gloves are made from. The condom rolls over a man's penis and is supposed to be left on the whole time the couple has sexual intercourse.

Condoms do two things when they work right: First, they catch the man's semen when he ejaculates so the woman should not get pregnant. Second, they prevent the skin of the man's penis from touching the inside of her vagina, which helps prevent germs from crossing from his body to hers or from her body to his.

Condoms do make sex physically safer—there's no disputing this fact. People who use condoms are significantly less likely to get pregnant or catch STIs than are people who have sex without using condoms. But how safe do condoms make sex?

Medical professionals who recommend condoms admit that condoms are less than perfect. These professionals extrapolate how well condoms work by estimating how often a couple who had sex regularly for one year would wind up with the woman pregnant. If that couple doesn't have sex at all, the chance of pregnancy would be zero percent. If they don't use a condom or any other method of birth control, their chance of pregnancy would be 85 percent. But if they're experienced at using condoms and use them regularly, their chance of pregnancy is about 15 percent. That's better than 85 percent, but there's still a significant chance of pregnancy.

Why aren't condoms completely effective? Sometimes they break. Sometimes they have tiny invisible holes big enough for germs and semen to get through. Also, condoms fail more often when used by teenagers than by adults because teenagers often don't use them correctly. While condoms are effective in stopping those diseases spread exclusively through semen and vaginal fluids, there are serious sexually transmitted diseases that condoms don't stop, such as HPV. HPV spreads over the skin, so while using a condom will stop HPV transmission through the skin of the penis, it will not stop *other* skin contact that can transmit HPV (like the man's scrotum touching the woman's labia during sex).

Is this safe enough? Imagine you have a three-year-old brother and you live near a big highway. Your brother says he wants to play on the highway, which you know would be deadly. Would you let him play there? Of course not. But suppose he asks that you let him play on the shoulder of the road, where the cars don't usually drive and it would be safer. Is that a good idea? Suppose he asks to play on the hill right next to the highway, where he might accidentally roll down the hill onto the shoulder of the road. Would this be all right because it's safer than playing on the highway or its shoulder? How safe is safe enough?

Safe sex? Or safer sex? Sex outside of marriage is physically safer if people use the pill or a condom, but they're still at risk for pregnancy and disease.

The physical consequences of sex outside of marriage—specifically pregnancy and disease—are very serious. These dangers make sense if God made sex only for marriage. One reason to save sex for marriage is to stop these bad things from happening to you. But this is not the most important reason not to have sex before you are married. That's our next subject!

CHAPTER 11

# *Saving Sex for Marriage: Thinking Biblically*

**THERE'S NOTHING WRONG** with thinking through practical reasons not to have sex, such as getting pregnant or catching an STI. The way the book of Proverbs discusses sex suggests that its author was aware of many bad consequences of sexual misbehavior (take a look at Proverbs 7).

The Bible also is full of stories about people who misused God's gift of sex and whose lives were devastated as a result. Perhaps the most infamous story is that of King David's sexual abuse and adultery with Bathsheba, which resulted in David indirectly murdering her husband, Uriah (the whole story is in 2 Samuel 11). The inclusion of these honest, heartbreaking stories suggests that God wants to teach us that obedience to him not only gives him glory but also helps us to live blessed lives.

In fact, God tells us that our obedience to his laws is good for us—there's nothing more practical than that! In Deuteronomy, God says his laws are given for our own good.

> And now, Israel, what does the LORD your God require of you, but to fear the LORD your God, to walk in all his ways, to love him, to serve the LORD your God with all your heart and with all your soul, and to keep the commandments and statutes of the LORD, which I am commanding you today *for your good*?
>
> DEUTERONOMY 10:12-13, EMPHASIS ADDED

The fact that sex is safer when people follow God's rules is the first of three great reasons to save sexual intercourse for when you're married. Now it's time to talk about the other two of those three great reasons: (1) People honor God by obeying him; and (2) when people obey him, they live in a way that matches with the very purpose and meaning of sex.

## HONORING GOD BY OBEYING HIM

A fundamental reason for not having sex outside of marriage is that God doesn't want you to. Jesus said, "If you love me, you will keep [obey] my commandments" (John 14:15). God wants you to show your love for him by the way you live your life.

You can honor God with your heart and mind by believing and trusting him. You honor God by using your body to do good things and not the things of which God disapproves. The Bible teaches that when people save sexual intercourse for marriage, they honor God with their bodies. Obedience is a way of showing love.

> Jesus said to him, "I am the way, and the truth, and the life. No one comes to the Father except through me. . . . If you love me, you will keep my commandments." . . . Jesus answered him, "If anyone loves me, he will keep my word, and my Father will love him, and we will come to him and make our home with him. Whoever does not love me does

> not keep my words. And the word that you hear is not mine but the Father's who sent me."
>
> JOHN 14:6, 15, 23-24

> Flee from sexual immorality. Every other sin a person commits is outside the body, but the sexually immoral person sins against his own body. Or do you not know that your body is a temple of the Holy Spirit within you, whom you have from God? You are not your own, for you were bought with a price. So glorify God in your body.
>
> 1 CORINTHIANS 6:18-20

The physical dangers of sex are only part of the story. Sex before marriage also puts you in spiritual danger. Why? Because obeying God helps people grow close to him, and disobeying God often causes people to drift away from him. Young people who misuse the gift of sexuality not only take physical risks but also gamble that they can disobey God and still stay in loving relationship with him.

> By this we know that we have come to know him, if we keep his commandments. Whoever says "I know him" but does not keep his commandments is a liar, and the truth is not in him, but whoever keeps his word, in him truly the love of God is perfected. By this we may know that we are in him: whoever says he abides in him ought to walk in the same way in which he walked.
>
> 1 JOHN 2:3-6

## HONORING THE VERY PURPOSE AND MEANING OF SEX

You have many big choices ahead of you, and one of the biggest is to decide what you believe about sex. Beyond the facts about people's bodies (which we talked about in chapters 4 through 8), *what do you believe sex is for, what does it mean, and how should it be used?*

Christians believe that God intentionally made the sexual parts of people's bodies to be wonderfully sensitive. He gave people the capacity for great pleasure. Of course, non-Christians also believe that human bodies are good and are able to give us great pleasure, but one way in which we Christians are different from people who don't believe in God is that Christians believe people's bodies are *gifts* from God, gifts husbands and wives are meant to give to each other on their wedding nights.

People treat gifts differently than they treat things they've made or bought. If you work to earn money and buy a game or piece of clothing, you may feel as if you can do anything you want with it—you may even give it away, lose it, or break it. But usually people don't feel that way about gifts. People see a gift as an expression of love and caring from another person. It's right to feel that way about the gift of sex.

It's important to think about how God wants you to use that gift. And without question, your future wife or husband would want you to give the gift of your body as something you have never shared with anyone else. In this way, staying sexually pure honors your future spouse as well as God.

Adults feel a special longing for someone special to love and be loved by for a lifetime. God made sexual intercourse to be a special "glue" that helps hold two people together for a lifelong marriage. When two people have sex, they become "one flesh." God said this about making the very first human beings: "Therefore a man shall leave his father and his mother and hold fast to his wife, and they shall become one flesh" (Genesis 2:24).

## TWO BECOME ONE?

What does it mean for two different people to become one flesh? Nobody fully understands this mystery. God doesn't give us the answer in the Bible. But even though it's a mystery, it's true—sex was meant to bond and keep on bonding two people together for life.

When a husband and wife have sexual intercourse, they completely share their bodies with each other. If they truly love each other and can share their lives with each other, then having sexual intercourse can truly be what people call it: "making love." The couple will have sex because they love each other, and they will love each other more because they have sex. They share their whole bodies because they share their whole selves. The Bible teaches us just how special this gift of sexual intercourse is.

God made sex to be a special connection between a husband and wife. They're joined in some mysterious way the Bible doesn't explain. *Sex is a life-uniting act.* It was meant to be used as a special gift in marriage, a way to help bond two people together for life.

Being united with and faithful to your spouse for life honors God because it shows the whole world what his faithfulness looks like, which is God's purpose for marriage. Do you trust that God desires what's best for you? Do you trust that his design for sex is best for you? Doing as God commands honors him and fits with the way your heart is made to love.

If you use God's gift of sex for any other purpose than to build a strong marriage—if you use it to have fun or to prove that you're a real man or woman—you use the gift wrongly. Sex bonds two people together, like glue. Have you ever glued something together and realized later you made a mistake? You might get it apart, but the residue of the glue is always there, and it never goes back together right. Misusing God's gift of sex glues you to the wrong person, and as a result you'll probably get hurt.

> Do you not know that your bodies are members of Christ? Shall I then take the members of Christ and make them members of a prostitute? Never! Or do you not know that

> he who is joined to a prostitute becomes one body with her? For, as it is written, "The two will become one flesh."
>
> 1 CORINTHIANS 6:15-16

Sex outside of marriage hurts people not only physically and spiritually but also emotionally. Because sexual intimacy unites two people, sexual intercourse with the wrong person can cause emotional damage. Mike feels that because he had sex before marriage, it's harder for him to feel bonded to his wife. Kristin feels as if a piece of her heart was broken to pieces because she had sex with her boyfriend, who later broke up with her.

*Scientific studies show that people who had less sex before marriage are happier with their marriages, enjoy sex more in their marriages, and divorce less frequently than people who had more sex before they were married.*

We believe that sex before marriage is one reason why so many people find it hard to have good, lifelong marriages. Many more people have sex before marriage now than used to be the case. As the number of people who have had sex before marriage has gone up, so has the rate of divorce.

By having sex with people other than their husbands or wives, people may be breaking down their abilities to unite with those they marry. If a person who has had sex outside of marriage is really sorry and asks God for forgiveness and healing, God can and will help that person. But shouldn't you protect yourself from this kind of damage in the first place?

### HOW UNITED IS UNITED?

Being united—or being one flesh—with your husband or wife is a complicated thing. We (Stan and Brenna) had sexual intercourse for our first time on the night we were married. It's true to say that we became one flesh that day after exchanging our vows, celebrating our marriage, and making love for the first time that night. But there's a sense in which being one flesh is something we're still working on. We'll always be working on it. Sex is a vitally important part—but it is only part—of becoming one.

Sex does bond two people together, as the Bible teaches, but this doesn't mean that any two people who have sex are married or must stay together. A person who has had sex with ten people in the past is not married to all of those people. And people who have sex as teenagers shouldn't feel they must marry their sexual partners. Marriages that start out this way often end in divorce and disaster.

People who have had sex before marriage should commit themselves to not having sex again before they marry. They should pray that God would forgive them for breaking his rules, heal them from the hurt and the damage done, and release them from the effects of joining themselves to people they weren't married to.

## PUTTING IT TOGETHER

Saving sex for marriage is the best thing you can do spiritually and practically. Look deep in your heart. Which of the following two scenarios sounds like the wiser choice?

First scenario: Before you're married, you have sex with three or more people you have some affection for, and then you try to forge a true sense of being "one flesh" with your new wife or husband.

Second scenario: You find one person you truly love, and you marry and stay bonded to this person for life, sharing the full intimacy of your bodies, having and raising children together until death parts you.

Only the second scenario meets the clear standards of Scripture as God's chosen path, a path he delights in and promises to bless. This scenario also helps you avoid STIs, pregnancy before marriage, and the emotional and relational damages caused by sex before marriage. Saving sex for marriage is definitely the wiser choice.

### THE LIES YOU WILL HEAR

Let's see how the false claims about sex you'll hear at school and other places stand up under closer scrutiny.

1. "Sex is the very best way to express affection and love. If you really love someone, you'll have sex." Everyone has heard this claim in various forms. But the truth is you don't have to have sex before marriage to express true affection. Instead, take time to really get to know and love the person you're growing to love. You don't have to have sex to express love. You can express your love for each other through kindness and thoughtfulness and by enjoying all the good and wonderful things about the person you love.

2. "You must have sex to be a normal, mature, grown-up person." Really, who is the mature person? The person who goes along with the crowd and believes what social media, television, and movies tell her to believe? Or the person who believes God and the Bible? Is it the person who has the strength to do what is right even when people around him do not? The Bible says a mature person has self-control and knows that loving and obeying God is important. A mature person doesn't need to have sex before marriage.

3. "The desire for sex is so strong it cannot be resisted." Really? Jesus lived for thirty-three years and never had sex. Millions of single Christians have lived their lives and never had sex, while millions of others have waited for many years and saved sex for marriage. It's a lie that we must have sex.

4. "It's important to try sex before you get married to make sure you're sexually compatible." This is terrible advice. There's no special, magical way two bodies fit together that makes sex great—you don't have to "shop around" and have sex with twenty people to find the best fit. "Sexual compatibility"—having a sexual relationship full of joy, pleasure, and beauty—develops out of the quality of the love a couple shares and out of their desire to please each other.

   A loving married couple creates sexual compatibility by learning how to please each other better the longer they live together. Two people who truly love each other will work to improve their sexual relationship over the years of their marriage so their joy with each other can grow more and more.

5. "It's important to have sex to practice for marriage." Not so. The couple who saves sex for marriage can have the joy of practicing and learning to love each other better together. Scientific studies show that having sex with lots of people before marriage is associated with less happy marriages, more divorces, and less happiness with sex in marriage. This is evidence that people who live by God's rules are more likely to have better marriages and better sex lives.

6. "Sex is always good." Was sex good for the thousands of people who now have sexually transmitted diseases, including HIV and AIDS? Was sex good for the almost one million teenage girls who got pregnant last year? Was it good for the more than half a million babies born to unmarried teenage girls? Or for the more than 250,000 babies who were aborted by their mothers? Was it good for the girls who had sex because their boyfriends lied and claimed to love them and a month later moved on to other girls? Sexual intercourse is not always good.

### WHY SOME PEOPLE CHOOSE SEX BEFORE MARRIAGE

Given these reasons, why would anyone choose sex before marriage?

*Pleasure.* Some people have sex simply for the pleasure of it. Is this a good reason? No.

First, for women especially, it takes the love, respect, and partnership of marriage for sex to be its best. Many young women who have sex as teenagers have neutral or unpleasant experiences with sex because it happens without the love and commitment that marriage provides.

Second, many people seek the pleasure of sex because they have no purpose for their lives other than pleasure. Their lives lack higher purposes such as loving, serving, and worshiping God. For these people, having sex is a way they try to fill up an empty space in their lives. But only the love of Christ can fill up this space in people's lives. God made sex for a man and woman to enjoy in their marriage as a blessing, not as something for people to play around with on dates with those they hardly know.

*Loneliness.* Some people have sex because they're terribly, profoundly lonely. Girls without deep friendships with other girls may have sex with boys in order to make boys more interested in them. It's as if they're buying friendship with guys by having sex. Lonely guys do the same with girls.

Having sex can make you feel close for a few minutes, but it doesn't satisfy the way real love can. Lonely people need the real love of good friendships and the kind of real romantic love that waits until after marriage to have sex. Most important, lonely people need to find out how the love of God can fill their hearts. Sex is not the medicine to heal a lonely person's hurts.

Some young women think that having a baby will cure their loneliness. This almost always results in disaster. Sure, the baby will love its mother. But that love comes with a very high price. Raising a baby is really hard work, even for two parents, as they feed, change, and care for the tiny new life nonstop for days and weeks and months.

Having a baby will also change the girl's life forever, pulling her away from friends and making it harder to meet a man who can be her husband. The mother often winds up even more lonely.

*Pressure.* The teenage years are a time when it's painful not to be liked by all of your "friends," a time of wanting to fit in. Why is this?

During your teen years you're becoming your own person separate from your family. Having close friends during these years keeps you from feeling so glued to your family and gives you a sense of being a different and unique person. You are no longer just a child in your family; you are your own person. But you don't become your own person by doing whatever your peer group does.

If you're a teenager in a group of friends who are having sex, you may be teased and pressured to lose your virginity. And sometimes teens can be ruthless. Getting clobbered on social media has hurt some teens so badly that they think about or attempt suicide. But when people have sex because they feel pressured to, it doesn't make anyone like them or love them more. It only shows that perhaps they don't have the strength to stand on their own to do what's right.

Pressure can come from friends or from romantic interests. Girls can pressure guys, and guys can pressure girls. They may ask, beg, or demand to have sex, saying things like "I just want us to be closer in our love" or "If we don't have sex, I'm going to explode" or "You say you love me, but the real proof of love is making love." Some people struggle to stand up to this pressure, so they choose to have sex.

> We are his workmanship, created in Christ Jesus for good works, which God prepared beforehand, that we should walk in them.
>
> EPHESIANS 2:10

It's better if we're not alone. We feel stronger when we know others who agree with us. And we're never alone if we're doing what is right, because Jesus stands with us. With God on our side, we can stand against anything. "If God is for us, who can be against us?" (Romans 8:31).

But even when Christ is for us, it helps to have another person beside us. That's the reason it's important to be part of a church youth group or a Christian group that prays or studies the Bible. You'll be better prepared to stand against the pressure of other kids when you have friends who believe as you do. "Do not be deceived: 'Bad company ruins good morals'" (1 Corinthians 15:33), but "Though a man might prevail against one who is alone, two will withstand him—a threefold cord is not quickly broken" (Ecclesiastes 4:12).

*Insecurity.* Some people don't have a firm idea of what they believe or what kinds of people they are, so they can't feel good about who they are. They try to find ways to feel better about themselves, such as by having other people tell them that they're liked or that they've passed some kind of test that makes them fit in. Insecure people may give in to sex so other people will say they're cool or okay. It's a terrible idea to have sex to try to earn others' approval. Having sex for this reason proves nothing about people except, perhaps, that they're foolish and weak.

There are no valid reasons for having sex outside of marriage. The only good and perfect reason to have sex is to express joy and pleasure in your husband or wife and to build a lifetime union in marriage.

## SUMMING IT UP

Lies about sex will come from every direction. By saving sexual intercourse for marriage, you will please God by your obedience; you will protect yourself against physical diseases, pregnancy, and emotional pain; and you will prepare yourself to build a marriage of real unity and love.

You may feel you're too young to make such big decisions about your life, but you're not! Now is the right time to think and pray about these matters and to decide which way your life will go.

## CHAPTER 12

# *Love before Marriage*

**BEFORE YOU GO** through puberty, you may think about love, but you won't feel powerfully drawn to it. But after puberty you can experience powerful yearnings for a special relationship as well as new and unsettling feelings of excitement and desire. Love and sex begin to sound wonderful.

The same hormones that cause your body to mature also change your brain and the way your mind and feelings work, including how you feel about love and sex. But there's more: The way you think about love and sex changes as you mature. Part of being a child is being dependent on your parents. Part of being an adult, on the other hand, is being independent and starting a family of your own. To do that, you need a love relationship with one special person from outside your family.

Feeling sexual desire and love is part of the normal process of physically and emotionally maturing and of becoming independent of your family. God wants you to grow up and feel those things because it's part of his plan for you as an adult.

In this chapter, we discuss the sorts of relationships you might have in which you can learn about, experience, and enjoy such feelings in ways that help and do not hurt you, and in ways that honor God. In the next chapter, we discuss what kinds of sexual behaviors might take place in such relationships.

## IT'S A DATE!

For many young people today, dating is an unknown concept. But in some form or another, men and women form romantic and sexual relationships, some of which end and some of which lead to marriage. It looks different in different parts of the world and in different groups of people, and it keeps changing.

In this chapter and the next, we lump all romantic and sexual relationships into what we are calling *dating*. The real question we want to ask here is *How do you handle romantic feelings and sexual feelings before marriage?* We are defining dating as whatever happens as a young man and woman get to know each other at deeper and deeper levels, how couples act who might be in love or falling in love, and how they handle those feelings and their sexual desires for each other before marriage.

## AM I READY FOR ROMANCE AND LOVE?

How do you get to know another? How do you move from meeting to true love and full intimacy? The process of getting to know another person doesn't happen just when you have time alone. One of the best ways to get to know another person when you're fourteen or fifteen is to have that person join your group of friends in a church or school group activity. This can be an opportunity to find out what kind of person he or she is without a lot of pressure or expectations.

Be cautious about what we call *independent dating*. We suggest you wait until you're at least sixteen before you experience emotionally or romantically intense time alone with your boyfriend or girlfriend. This should be approached with caution. By waiting until you're sixteen, you'll have more confidence in your ability to take care of yourself, since you'll be old enough to drive and get a job. You also will have had some experience in handling yourself in challenging situations, so if something isn't right, you can take care of yourself.

There's nothing magical about turning sixteen, however. Some will be ready at this time, some will have been ready before, and some will not be ready yet. Here are some helpful questions you may be able to discuss with your parents and trusted friends to get some clues as to whether or not you're ready for dating:

- *Do I feel good about myself? Am I confident? Do I have healthy self-esteem?* Dating is full of emotional twists and turns, high points and low points—you need to be ready to be bounced around a bit before you start dating.
- *Am I strong enough to say no? Do I have the strength to state and defend my own values, beliefs, and opinions? Can I set and defend my own boundaries? Am I willing to say no to something if it could result in me getting trashed on social media, rejected by false friends, or even worse?*
- *Do I have the strength and resilience to accept rejection?* That's what it feels like when someone you care for and thought you understood pulls away from you or pushes you away. And what about the reverse: *Do I have the capacity to be gracious in ending a relationship with another who isn't right for me?* That's what you'll need to do if you realize the other person isn't for you but he or she wants to keep dating.

- *What are my standards for agreeing to a date? What am I willing and not willing to do with the person I'm dating? How far am I willing to go physically?* (We discuss this later.) *What if the person wants to drink alcohol or do drugs? Do risky things such as driving too fast, taking dares, mingling with strangers in unfamiliar places? How will I make sure I don't get into a difficult situation?*

These are hard questions to ask and even harder questions to answer. Some of these questions can only be answered when you're faced with the actual situation, but you'll encounter real challenges when you date, and it's important to think about this ahead of time.

## DOES IT MATTER WHO I DATE?

The Bible instructs us that it's not wise for a Christian to marry someone who isn't a Christian. Why? Most married people discover it is vitally important that both partners in the marriage look at life in similar ways. It adds strength to your marriage if you both believe in God, can pray together, value the same things in life, believe the same things are right and wrong, and can enjoy serving and worshiping God together in your church. Couples who don't have a common bond of faith often find that their different views of God slowly become more painful and difficult to navigate, especially after they have children.

> Do not be unequally yoked with unbelievers. For what partnership has righteousness with lawlessness? Or what fellowship has light with darkness?
>
> 2 CORINTHIANS 6:14

We believe it's very important for Christians to date only other Christians. Friendships with non-Christians are good, but if friendship begins to grow toward something else—something romantic—be careful. Dating a person who does not share your faith likely will make your faith grow weaker, and the weaker your faith becomes, the poorer the choices you might make. If the other person is a Christian, you have a good foundation on which to get to know that person further.

## HE LOVES ME—HE LOVES ME NOT

One of the most frightening, wonderful, confusing, and joyous experiences of the teenage years is falling in love.

These feelings come in so many different varieties they're hard to describe. When you're just beginning to be interested in the opposite sex, you may find yourself thinking that a certain person is especially nice. You may feel as if you want to do things for that person, and you want that person to be a special friend. When these feelings grow stronger, you can get pretty swept away by them. Some teenagers find themselves thinking about special people all the time.

Especially in the early teenage years, some kids love to tease people who have romantic feelings toward others. Someone may taunt you with embarrassing questions or crude comments if they learn you're "in love" with someone.

Sometimes grown-ups aren't much better. They can be insensitive about what you feel. Your parents might call those feelings "puppy love" or some other name that implies they aren't real. Your parents might even say, "Oh, you aren't really in love." This kind of reaction by adults is understandable because, believe it or not, your parents and all of the adults around you have had the same feelings. Most parents who see their children going through the process of being "head over heels in love" remember how they had similar feelings at your age and how those relationships almost always ended in disappointment. This can make parents a little skeptical about your feelings.

Do you want to find out something new about your parents? Talk to them about the times they were in love when they were teenagers. Ask them to tell you how they felt and what kind of things they did as a result of feeling as if they were in love. Get them to tell you about the times they "went out" with someone, about the silliest things they did to express their affection, about what it felt like to be in love, and also what it felt like when a relationship broke up.

While a skeptical adult reaction is understandable, it's also unfortunate. A teenager's feelings should be treated with respect and care. God made you capable of feeling strong affection, and that's a very special gift from God.

## TAKE THE TEST

But even if those feelings are real and a gift from God, that doesn't mean the love you feel when you're thirteen or sixteen or nineteen is a mature love. There are only two tests that will show whether love is mature or not.

The first is the test of time. We remember times from our teenage years when we felt passionately, wildly, almost crazily in love with another person—and two weeks later we no longer had those feelings. A love that's true will stand the test of time as you get to know the other person better and better. True love finds out more of who the other person really is and grows to appreciate more and more about that person.

The second test of mature love is the test of restraint. A love that is true will grow slowly over time as the couple acts toward each other in the way God wants them to. Having too much of a physical relationship can actually prevent you from getting to know each other better. Too many couples step over the boundaries that they set, which creates guilt they must work through with each other and with God. This also creates emotional and spiritual confusion that becomes the focus of the relationship—it takes the place of the couple using their time and energy to really get to know each other at a deep level. It's much better to exercise restraint by honoring and living within the boundaries you set.

### SOME GOOD ADVICE ABOUT DATING

- Keep your other friendships going while you're dating—don't depend on dating as your only kind of friendship.
- Don't start dating too early. You have plenty of time to learn about love, so take your time.
- Ease gradually into dating as you're ready and as your parents agree you're ready.
- Relax. Enjoy a friendship rather than pursuing your possible spouse.
- Date only Christians. Your companions will affect who you are.
- Be accountable to your parents or other appropriate adult mentors for definite plans for dates. Do what you say you will do.
- When you're on a date, avoid movies and TV shows that focus on sex or that aim to get viewers sexually excited.
- Dress modestly for a date. Don't send out mixed signals.
- Involve the person you date in the important parts of your life, such as family gatherings and church activities.
- Be prepared to talk openly with the person you're dating about your moral standards regarding sex.
- Pray about your relationship and activities. Consider praying with a parent or trusted adult—ask God to honor and protect your relationship with the person you're dating.

## CHAPTER 13

# *How Far Should I Go?*

**PART OF HOW PEOPLE** feel about sex and love is connected to how they feel about other people's bodies. Before people go through puberty, most have a child's curiosity about others' bodies. But after puberty, people's interests in other bodies are more than just curiosity—they can include powerful feelings of excitement and desire.

Feelings of sexual desire are connected to romantic love. God made us so that the more love and infatuation we have, the more sexual feelings and desire we experience. Young children love their families and naturally desire to hug, kiss, and touch them. This is a way children express love with their bodies.

The attraction and love you experience as a teenager include this desire to hug or kiss, but the feelings are different and stronger. You may have noticed that couples who seem to be in love touch each other a lot, hold hands, and put their arms around each other. Some moms and dads act this way toward each other: They hug and kiss their children, but the hugs, kisses, and pats they give each other are different from those they give their children.

God made us so that we have sexual feelings about the people we romantically love. When a fourteen-year-old boy thinks about the girl he has feelings of love for, he may find himself with an erection—a sign of sexual excitement. A fourteen-year-old girl may notice a slight wetness in her vagina when she thinks about a boy she's attracted to.

This does not mean these teens are thinking about sexual intercourse or even about another person's body—it only means that God made people so that our feelings of love and attraction are connected with how our bodies respond sexually. This connection is a great gift; later, if you get married, your sexual relationship with your wife or husband will be a wonderful way for you to express your love.

After you go through puberty, you'll begin to respond to feelings of love as a whole person (body, mind, emotions, and spirit), as an adult. This is something to celebrate and not to be embarrassed about or feel guilty about.

## LOVE AND SEXUAL DESIRE

All these feelings—including the feeling that having sexual intercourse with someone would be wonderful—are part of a natural response to love. But many teenagers today wrongly believe that if someone experiences a sexual urge that seems fun or exciting, that person should go ahead and do it.

Wanting something doesn't mean it's right to have it. It's a good gift from God when a teenage couple in love are excited by each other and desire each other, but God doesn't want them to choose to have sex. As we discussed in chapters 10 and 11, sexual intercourse is to be reserved for marriage.

Our question here is *Are there ways people can express affection or be sexual in dating that are okay in God's eyes?*

## TO TOUCH OR NOT TO TOUCH

This is a difficult question, partly because the Bible doesn't talk directly about these things. Is that because God doesn't care what we do as long as we don't have sexual intercourse? No.

The Bible doesn't directly talk about this subject because dating as we know it today didn't exist when the Bible was written. Back then most people lived in very small towns and villages. Even the large cities of ancient Palestine were small by today's standards. Many marriages were arranged, which means that parents would make the decisions about who their children would marry. Unmarried men and women weren't left alone together because it was important to everyone that they not have sex before they were married. They had none of the privacy young couples have today. In that ancient culture, God didn't need to speak of rules for how people should behave when they dated, because they didn't date.

But the Bible offers good principles to guide you in your moral choices. To apply that advice to dating, we have to be clear about what can happen sexually in dating. Human beings have been very creative in what they do for sexual excitement and to make their bodies feel good sexually. A couple might hold hands or put their arms around each other. Even a simple touch on the shoulder or pat on the back can feel exciting if the person who touches you is someone you like or love.

## WHAT CAN HAPPEN

It's very common for couples to kiss when they have feelings of love for each other. But there are kisses and then there are *kisses*. A kiss may be a simple peck on the cheek or the lips. Or instead of a quick peck, the couple may kiss for a little bit longer.

Then there's the passionate kissing you may have seen on television or in the movies—during these kisses the couple seems stuck together for minutes. This kind of kissing is called French—or deep—kissing. In this kind of kissing, the man and woman open their lips and touch their tongues together as well as their lips. Our advice is to save such kisses for a very special person.

In spite of what happens in movies and on TV shows, most couples don't go directly from passionate kissing to having sexual intercourse. Some couples who are very attracted to each other gradually share more and more of their bodies with each other without having sexual intercourse. When someone has strong feelings of love for another person, it's natural to want to touch the other person's body, including the private parts—the woman's breasts and both partners' genitals.

When you let someone touch your private parts through your clothes or when you touch someone else's private parts, you're doing something much more intimate than just kissing. The intimacy becomes even greater if the couple begins to unbutton or take off their clothes so they're sharing more of their bodies. Instead of touching the other person through their clothes, they may directly touch the other person's uncovered breasts or genitals.

Such touching can be more or less intimate. A young man may briefly touch a young woman's crotch while she's wearing jeans, and while this is intimate, it's less intimate than if she lets him directly touch her genitals. Some couples touch each other's genitals—the girl rubs the boy's penis and the boy touches her vagina and clitoris—to the point of one or both of them having an orgasm. This is even more intimate, yet they haven't had sexual intercourse.

One of the most intimate things a couple can do without having actual intercourse is called *oral sex* (*oral* for "with the mouth"). A girl performs oral sex when she takes the boy's penis in her mouth and rubs it with her tongue and lips until he has an orgasm. A boy can perform oral sex on a girl by using his tongue and lips to caress her vagina and clitoris. In some teenage circles today, oral sex is becoming more common and isn't regarded as "having sex."

There are other and more twisted ways people engage in sexual acts. We call all of this *sexual intimacy*. You can see how, as a couple goes from kissing to intimate touching to oral sex and even beyond, the intimacy gets deeper and deeper and that they share more and more of their bodies.

## BIBLICAL GUIDANCE

What does God think of such sexual intimacy? The Bible gives us guidance, specifically some positive principles and some warnings.

> For this is the will of God, your sanctification: that you abstain from sexual immorality; that each one of you know how to control his own body in holiness and honor, not in the passion of lust like the Gentiles who do not know God. . . . For God has not called us for impurity, but in holiness. Therefore whoever disregards this, disregards not man but God, who gives his Holy Spirit to you.
>
> 1 THESSALONIANS 4:3-5, 7-8

> "All things are lawful for me," but not all things are helpful. "All things are lawful for me," but I will not be dominated by anything. . . . The body is not meant for sexual immorality, but for the Lord, and the Lord for the body. . . . Flee from sexual immorality. Every other sin a person commits is outside the body, but the sexually immoral person sins against his own body. Or do you not know that your body is a temple of the Holy Spirit within you, whom you have from God? You are not your own, for you were bought with a price. So glorify God in your body.
>
> 1 CORINTHIANS 6:12-13, 18-20

In the passages you just read, you can see the following:

- Your body is meant for the Lord; it is the Lord's. In fact, your body is his temple.
- Where there are not explicit laws in the Bible, you are still to pursue what is helpful and good and are not to be dominated by anything.
- You are to flee sexual immorality—to stay as far from it as possible (as opposed to pushing the boundaries by asking what the limits are so you can stop just short of breaking the rules).
- You should seek to glorify God in your body—to act with your body in ways that give glory to God.
- You should know how to control yourself and do so.
- You should pursue honor and holiness.

These are only two of the many places in the Bible where God says people should avoid sexual sin and pursue purity. In these passages the apostle Paul shows two basic ways to live your life. One way God calls holy, honorable, and pure—this way of life requires honoring God with your body and staying away from sinful sex. The other way Paul calls lustful, dishonorable, and impure—this is how God looks at sexual sin.

In Matthew 5:27-30 we read another important principle that Jesus shared. He affirmed that people shouldn't have sex with those they're not married to but then went on to say, "I say to you that everyone who looks at a woman with lustful intent has already committed adultery with her in his heart" (verse 28). From this, we draw our final principle: What you do with your thoughts is as important as what you do with your body. Beyond just keeping your body from doing things that break God's rules, you should also push back on desires or thoughts about breaking God's rules. Such thoughts go beyond simply recognizing the beauty or even sexual attractiveness of another person—these kinds of thoughts are natural, and to attempt to suppress them is likely to lead to compulsive preoccupation with them. We instead are talking about thoughts that go beyond noticing the attractiveness of another person in order to indulge in fantasies and preoccupations that misuse the person in your mind.

## WHAT IS SEX?

Putting this all together, we want to argue first that the reason the Bible says not to have sexual intercourse outside of marriage is to protect you against being bonded or glued to someone you're not married to. Sexual intercourse provides that special kind of bonding.

People who don't have sexual intercourse but engage in extensive sexual intimacy often experience some of this kind of bonding because they're essentially sharing all of their bodies with others as people do in sexual intercourse. Those who engage in intimate touching and oral sex commonly find there's very little left of their bodies they haven't shared.

If someone engages in full sexual intimacy—particularly direct touching of the genitals or oral sex—that person is at risk of getting the same sexually transmitted diseases that are transmitted through sexual intercourse. Anytime the body's sexual fluids—semen or vaginal lubrication—come in contact with another person, such transmission can occur. With more teenagers engaging in oral sex, sexually transmitted diseases of the mouth are becoming more common. These possibilities support viewing sexual touching of all kinds as sexual intimacy.

Such sexual intimacy can be dangerous simply because people who do it get very sexually excited, and when they're excited they don't make good decisions. A teenager may feel confident that she shouldn't have intercourse, but if she begins to have greater intimacy with her boyfriend, she may find herself thinking, *This is so exciting—I bet I can handle a bit more . . . and a bit more than that* . . . Many teens who wind up having sexual intercourse weren't planning to do so before they began to be more and more sexually intimate.

## STRAIGHT ADVICE

Together, these principles suggest that it's unwise for teenage couples to engage in sexual intimacy. When a couple becomes more sexually intimate, they encourage their hearts and minds to think about sex more and more. This can lead them into exactly the kind of lustful thoughts Jesus spoke against.

We want to summarize the advice we gave to our own children about what to share of their bodies in dating:

- The most important general rule is that *the more physical intimacy that is reserved for marriage, the better*. Some level of kissing and physical affection can be important when a dating relationship is serious, but it's easy to go too far and very hard to pull back on physical intimacy once a boundary is passed.
- Don't go on solitary dates until you're sixteen or older. When you're fifteen (or possibly fourteen, if your parents consent), group activities are a safer alternative.
- Be cautious about physical touching in any other way than very public and casual gestures such as pats on the back until you've known the other person well for a significant amount of time (at least several months—talk with a parent or trusted, mature adult about this).
- Save intimate, deep kissing until your dating relationship has been exclusive and positive for a significant amount of time. Your level of emotional intimacy and knowledge of your love interest should far exceed your physical intimacy.

- If you're dating seriously, explicitly talk about your physical relationship, commit your thoughts to God in prayer, and set your standards and live by them.
- Any further physical intimacy should be reserved for an older age (twenty or older), after engagement or serious declarations of the intent to get engaged.
- Even in engagement, direct touching of the genitals of either person is sexual intimacy of which God would likely not approve and that you could later regret.

Our goal in this chapter has been to empower you to think over and make a decision about what you will and will not do before you even start developing a close relationship with another person. We urge you to be careful with the precious gift of your sexual body and decide on your standards now.

> I have set before you life and death, blessing and curse. Therefore choose life, that you and your offspring may live, loving the LORD your God, obeying his voice and holding fast to him.
>
> DEUTERONOMY 30:19-20

## STANDING YOUR GROUND

You will experience pressure to go beyond your limits—even pressure to go "all the way." Handling pressure starts with deciding what you will and will not do. Decide now whether or not you'll have sex before you're married. Before you ever begin a romantic relationship, be confident about what level of sexual intimacy you will allow when dating. Don't wait until you're out on a date or at someone's house to decide. Talk with God about your decision. After you make a decision, tell God, your parents, and a Christian friend about that decision. It pleases God when his people make and keep promises to him.

> Choose this day whom you will serve. . . . But as for me and my house, we will serve the LORD.
>
> JOSHUA 24:15

Next, think through how you'll handle pressure. Most of this pressure will come in the form of comments such as the following:

- "What's the matter with you—are you a prude?"
- "Haven't you grown up yet—are you still a child?"
- "You say that you care for me, but you don't show it by doing what people who love each other do."
- "If you don't have sex with me, I'm going to ruin your reputation by telling everyone at school what a prude you are!"
- "You said you'd go out with me, and that means you'll have sex, so stop being a tease!"

It's not important that you have a snappy or clever answer to any of these comments. Say no in a way that indicates you really mean it. Don't get drawn into a debate—you have decision power over your body and your life. You can simply say, "I do not choose to have sex with you (or kiss you or let you touch me). I want to go home now; this date is over."

Pressure to have sex can sometimes get even worse. A number of girls report being forced to have sex on dates. Sometimes a girl may let herself be talked into having sex, or she may feel threatened by a boy who says he'll ruin her reputation or worse. Sexual abusers often "groom" their victims by slowly increasing the pressure to have greater and greater physical involvement. If you ever feel pressured in any way, immediately report it to a parent or adult. Young women need to be strong to handle these kinds of threats. If a person uses threats against you, immediately separate yourself from that person, and if you're on a date, find another way home.

Beware of the danger of any situation where alcohol is served. Women are much more likely to be pressured—verbally, emotionally, and physically—when alcohol is consumed by either of you. Alcohol lowers your inhibitions, often with bad results. Girls who are inexperienced drinkers often become more inebriated than they realize or intend, and many sexual assaults happen then. Of course, the perpetrator of sexual assault is always to blame for the assault, but it's wise for women to take precautions.

No one has the right to force you to do anything you don't want to do. Sex without full consent is rape. Most people who make the threats we mentioned above cannot carry them out, but if they actually do, the things they threaten are not nearly as bad as having sex—being raped—would be.

Threatening your assailant with criminal charges may help; the minimum age when young persons can grant consent legally is sixteen in the United States. In most states it's seventeen or eighteen, and someone older who has sex with a person younger than the age of consent legally has committed rape.

In extreme cases, you may have to fight back physically. God doesn't want you to be a victim. Slap the person, yell or scream, poke him in the eye, twist his finger until it breaks—these may seem like intense actions, but they could help you safely get out of an out-of-control situation.

We know it can be scary to talk about these things, but by having a clear idea about what you should and shouldn't do, you can protect yourself and keep yourself safe. And the best way to lower the chances of this ever happening is to know the person you're with, make it clear what your standards are, be sure he's a Christian, and have safe plans for your time together.

## FINAL THOUGHTS

By choosing not to have sexual intercourse with anyone before you marry and by choosing to keep your body private and special by not engaging in intimate touching, you honor God. You make the gift of your body that much more special for the person you may someday marry. And if you stay single, you're protecting yourself from possible problems and are giving the gift of your body to God, just like he wants (see Romans 12:1-2).

## CHAPTER 14

# *Solitary Sex*

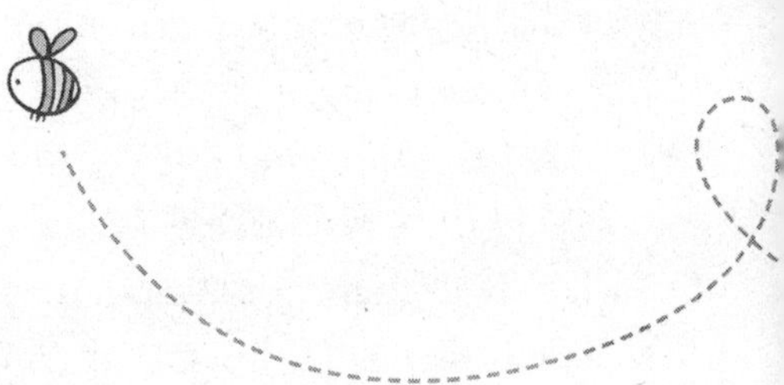

**YOU'VE PROBABLY HEARD** jokes about masturbation, but maybe you don't know what it is. *Masturbation* refers to people experiencing sexual pleasure by touching their own sexual organs. Sometimes people engage in casual touching just for the way it feels, but other times people masturbate in order to produce orgasm or climax.

Boys engage in masturbation more often than girls do, perhaps in part because boys grow up handling their penises when they bathe or urinate. This makes them more aware of how it can feel good when they touch themselves. Many girls are less aware of the good feelings possible from their clitorises, labia, and vaginas because they have fewer occasions to touch themselves directly and because of the private location of their genitals.

**Masturbation** *refers to people giving themselves sexual pleasure by touching their own sexual organs.*

Most boys have tried masturbation at least a few times by the age of sixteen. Many masturbate to the point of having orgasms and ejaculations. Some girls try masturbation, and some do it regularly, including having orgasms.

### THE ALLURE OF PROMISCUITY

This is an appropriate place to discuss a special form of brokenness that tends to affect men more than women. It's the allure of sexual novelty.

Scientific studies have found that men experience sexual desire and attraction across a wide range of women they encounter. The average man not constrained by love for God, love for his wife or future wife, his moral commitments, or his circumstances (or some combination of these) would pursue sex with a wide array of women.

Some women have an inclination toward promiscuity (having many sexual partners), but this is unusual. Women feel deeply in their bodies the connection of sex to the possibility of life and family. Young men feel the same desires for faithful love and the possibility of family but with much more conflict with their promiscuous urges.

A famous psychological experiment illustrates this. Attractive male and female actors went up to random people of the opposite sex on a college campus, introduced themselves, and then said something like "I've noticed you around campus and find you attractive. Would you like to get coffee?" In response to this question, about half the women and half the men who were approached said yes, they would be open to coffee.

With a separate group of random people, the actors changed the script just slightly. This time they said, "I've noticed you around campus and find you attractive. Would you like to come to my apartment tonight so we can get to know each other?"

The responses of men and women receiving this invitation were very different. When it was a male actor asking a young woman to come to his apartment, the women mostly said they were not interested—on average, fewer than 10 percent of women said yes. But the reaction was the opposite for young men: When the female actor offered this, about 70 percent of men said yes.

The experimenters had one more version of the script. This time, the actors said, "I . . . find you attractive. Would you have sex with me tonight?" Very consistently, women said, "No way!" to such a crude solicitation. This experiment has been repeated with thousands, and almost no women have said yes.

But the average percentage of men who say, "Absolutely—yes!" consistently is more than 80 to 85 percent.

We believe there's a lesson here: Men and women both have twisted and broken aspects of their sexuality. Each individual is unique with his or her own struggles. But generally speaking, most women instinctively connect sex with marriage and family. As a result, they're repulsed by promiscuity and yearn for one true love with whom to share their bodies.

Men, on the other hand, live with a constant battle between a desire for one true love and an attraction to sexual promiscuity (a pull toward sex with many people, regardless of affection and love). This tendency presents a special danger when it comes to thinking about masturbation.

## THINKING IT THROUGH

As Christians, how should we think about masturbation?

Many Christian young people feel horribly guilty about masturbation. In some churches, masturbation is discussed as if it were the ultimate evil act and deeply abnormal. Outside of religious circles, many people think that masturbation is no big deal because it's done in private, doesn't pass diseases or cause any other physical problems, and doesn't cause pregnancies.

The Bible doesn't seem to talk specifically about it. It does seem that if masturbation were a horrible evil in God's eyes, it would be specifically named and condemned in the Bible. But it isn't. So is it okay?

While the Bible doesn't talk about masturbation, the Lord Jesus teaches that what we do with our minds is as important as what we do with our bodies. Jesus condemns lust (see Matthew 5:28). He says committing adultery with our bodies is wrong *and* that committing adultery in our hearts is wrong also.

Lust is more than noticing that someone is attractive—it's using our minds to imagine sex that God would say is wrong. For example, a woman imagining sex with her husband would not be lusting, since God smiles on her love relationship with him. But for her to imagine having a sexual affair with her next-door neighbor would be lust, because God would not approve of that relationship.

Many young people who masturbate don't just touch themselves—they also imagine sexual ideas and pictures, such as having sex with classmates. The command of Jesus not to let lust dominate our lives probably means that masturbation isn't a wise practice. Masturbation while looking at pornography is very clearly a deliberate act of lust that can be very destructive (we talk about this in the next chapter).

**Lust:** *using people in our minds as sexual objects of pleasure in any way that would be wrong if that same behavior were really to happen*

There are other reasons to be cautious about masturbation. Masturbation is incomplete; it's not the full blessing God wants for your sexuality. God made your sexual feelings and your body for a very special purpose: to be *shared* with your life partner in marriage. Because masturbation is something a person does alone rather than with a spouse, it can be selfish rather than loving. So even though masturbation may sometimes feel physically good, it will never feel complete.

Finally, habitual and frequent masturbation can become a problem because it forms habits of feeling pleasure that make the focus your own touch and patterns of self-pleasuring. This is not what God desires. He made your sexuality to be linked to the beautiful and unique body of your future spouse, not to your own pleasure. Masturbation can set up expectations that interfere with your enjoyment of your husband or wife.

## CONCLUSION

Habitual and frequent masturbation associated with use of pornography certainly grieves God's heart and is a terrible misuse of the gift of our sexuality. Masturbation dominated by lust is a practice that pulls you away from the purity that God seeks in your heart.

On the other hand, occasional masturbation that focuses on the pleasure of your body or the release of sexual tension—but not on lustful images—may not be much of an issue with God. There may be more harm done by people punishing themselves with extreme guilt than by the masturbation. We don't think God wants his children to be overwhelmed with or obsessed about it.

# CHAPTER 15

# *Slaves to a False Image*

SLAVERY IS A THING of the past, right? Didn't it end in America more than 150 years ago when President Lincoln set the slaves free?

Slavery is alive and well in the world, including in America. One way slavery still exists today is through sex trafficking. Sex trafficking is when adults or children are torn from their families and communities and sold into slavery for sexual purposes.

Can you imagine anything more horrifying than being kidnapped, taken to a strange country, and forced to have sex against your will? Boys and girls, women and men (mostly girls and women) are sold into service as prostitutes or as the sexual property of one person. Victims of sex trafficking often are forced to have sex with many other people. In addition, these acts are sometimes filmed and sold on the Internet. Such slavery is real.

An estimated twenty-one million people a year worldwide are bought and sold into slavery of various kinds. Most are probably sold as workers, but a significant portion are sold into sexual slavery. It happens right here in the United States.

Another common type of slavery in the United States is drug addiction. Teens who misuse prescription drugs or use illegal drugs take enormous risks. They obtain such drugs from criminals and then smoke, swallow, or inject substances without knowing what they're really getting. Huge numbers of teenagers and young adults become addicts to various kinds of illegal drugs. They're essentially slaves to their habits and slaves to those criminals who provide the drugs for them.

A third kind of slavery is a huge risk for young people today: addiction to *pornography* or "porn." Pornography comes in many forms but always presents sexually arousing material—such as actors engaged in various sexual acts—in order to catch your interest and draw you into viewing more porn. Later in this chapter, we'll discuss some ways in which pornography is connected to both sexual slavery and drug addiction.

## THE SALES PITCH

Some young people are tempted to sample pornography out of curiosity. They wonder, *What do other people's bodies really look like? Is how I look normal? What really happens when people have sex? Will seeing it make me better at sex when I'm ready?*

There are answers to these questions: Yes, you look normal—how you compare to others doesn't matter, because you are you. You know the essentials about sex from this book and from your parents, and any additional information you might learn from pornography is not worth the damage that occurs when someone watches other people have sex. Finally, exposure to porn will likely complicate and diminish your joy and blessing in learning about sex when you first marry.

We understand that you will need to trust us for these answers to satisfy your questions. The pressures to view pornography are powerful. Other kids might say stuff like the following:

- "Don't be a prude!"
- "This is the most fantastic thing ever!"
- "Nobody is hurt, so what's the problem?"
- "Are you some kind of robot to let your religion tell you what to do?"

There are other ways you'll experience pressure to view porn. Pornography is big business. It's estimated to be at least a $97 billion business worldwide. A lot of that money goes into enticing you to watch and buy the product.

A lot of pornography is free, but the goal is to get money from you. The free stuff is bait to hook you. With money at stake, pornographers use sophisticated technological methods to sell their product, such as pop-up ads on your computer screen, strange or fraudulent e-mails, and texts on your phone. These and many other methods push you to try it.

The temptation of pornography will hit you at your most vulnerable time. In the years after puberty, your sexual feelings are very strong and new. This pulls you toward looking at porn. The part of your brain that helps you say no will not be at its strongest until you are in your twenties, and it's not used to handling this new temptation.

It will require real determination for you to say no—but you can do it. But why should you say no?

### THINKING WITH "THE MIND OF CHRIST" (1 CORINTHIANS 2:16)

How does Christ want us to think about and respond to pornography?

- **Pornography violates the sacred privacy of individual bodies and intimate sexual acts.** Our bodies are the temples of the Holy

Spirit, and each person's sexuality is a divine gift God intends only to be given to a future spouse. A good test is to ask yourself the following question: *Would I be proud if my sister, my mother, or I were filmed and were viewed engaging in such behavior?*

- **Pornography violates and mocks the Christian virtue of modesty.** God designed each of us to share our bodies openly with one person. In contrast, through porn, a young man can see more "ideal" nude women and more vivid, intense, novel, and shocking sexual stimuli in one hour than ten adult men who lived one hundred years ago could have seen in their combined lifetimes. Men's brains were not designed for this any more than they were designed to handle heroin!

- **Pornography always depicts immoral acts and draws the viewer into them.** Pornography presents promiscuous and degrading sexual acts in ways that make them seem thrilling and alluring. The person who views pornography mentally participates in the very acts the apostle Paul told us to flee: "Flee from sexual immorality. Every other sin a person commits is outside the body, but the sexually immoral person sins against his own body" (1 Corinthians 6:18). Pornographic images arouse sexual desire and lust, especially in men because they're more visually oriented than women.

- **Pornography implants immoral images that are hard to erase.** One of the things that scientists have learned about memory is that some of the most powerful images that can be programmed into the brain are images linked with strong emotion and novelty. Sexually arousing pornographic images—especially those that are shocking or unique—are deeply implanted in the brain and are very difficult to ever eliminate. You're at a time in life when it's vital to be filling your teenage mind with what's good and true and holy (see Philippians 4:8-9); pornography programs the mind with what's evil and false and dirty.

- **Pornography implants unrealistic images**—it fails to depict honestly the discomfort, pain, or humiliation suffered by one or both participants or the use of drugs to enhance sexual performance or dull pain. These images will likely interfere with learning how to give and receive love physically with your future spouse.
- **Pornography almost universally presents a degrading, sexualized view of women.** The vast majority of pornography is targeted at men, and the female actors are paid or made to act essentially as sexual slaves doing whatever men fantasize. Pornography presents women's bodies as objects to be used by men. It dishonestly presents women desiring what for most women is abnormal and unwanted behavior. Hardcore pornography that presents women as the objects of violence, degradation, and torture is particularly repulsive.
- **Pornography encourages violence toward women.** The use of pressure, force, and even violence against women is common in pornography. Scientific studies have shown that men who watch such pornography tend to shift their attitudes toward believing that violence toward women is justified and acceptable.
- **Some pornography is produced using women in sexual slavery.** There are no hard statistics, but there can be no question that some female actors in pornographic films have been forced into some type of sexual slavery. This means that people who consume this pornography support this kind of abuse of women.
- **To make more money, pornographers try to draw you into watching more and more extreme and perverted sexual acts that will cost you more and more money at higher and higher risk.**

## THE DANGER OF SEXUAL ADDICTION

Not only is viewing pornography against God's moral laws, it's also dangerous, which makes sense because it violates God's intent for his gift of sex. Addiction to pornography is a true threat.

There's a growing movement today of men, young and old, coming forward and admitting that an addiction to pornography has consumed their lives. These men have spent hours and hours viewing and masturbating to pornography. As a result, they fail to form normal relationships with women, waste thousands and thousands of dollars, do poorly or fail at school, lose jobs, and even destroy their marriages. Some of these men who have been immersed in sexual images and arousal find that they can no longer function in real sexual relationships.

What does it mean to have a sexual addiction?

To understand the addiction, it's helpful to understand the way sexual intimacy is supposed to be. God designed our emotions and our brains in a way that supports family life as he intended: one man married to one woman, loving each other and loving their children through a lifelong union.

## WHAT GOD INTENDED

The following is God's plan for us: A man and a woman limit their sexual experience before they marry, and they focus on growing to know each other as friends and soul mates as they near their wedding day. They know each other at a deep level. While they have strong physical and sexual desires for each other, they know that they can wait because God has something great in store for them after they're married.

Scientists are beginning to understand how our brains respond to this. As a man and woman get to know each other better, their brains form rich brain connection networks supporting their abilities to understand each other. When they laugh and enjoy each other, chemical transmitters associated with pleasure and reward are released in their brains.

Exercising self-control in their physical lives encourages development of the front part of their brains, which is the seat of self-control and mature judgment. As the man and woman grow in love, more pleasure hormones are released, and so are the chemical transmitters associated with deep love and satisfaction. So godly love promotes maturity, steady pleasure, and love. This seems to be what our brains are designed to experience.

On their wedding day, the couple stand before family and friends and exchange vows of loyalty and faithfulness. They do so knowing they've lived loyally and faithfully to each other before they were married and even before they knew each other. This is a foundation of trust on which they can build loyalty to each other for life.

On their wedding night, they give their bodies to each other for the first time. Sure, there's some awkwardness since they've never had sexual intercourse before. But imagine the joy, the excitement, the mystery, and the pleasure in store for them in their first experience. Imagine the joy and the pleasure of learning to please each other better and better with no prior expectations, no pornographic images for comparison, and no guilt.

At the biological level, when these newlyweds share their first experiences of sexual intercourse, it sets off in their brains an explosion of the chemicals associated with pleasure, love, and bonding, which further cements their relationship. Their relationship continues to solidify, and the eventual addition of children further bonds them together in ever more powerful ways.

## ADDICTION: WHEN IT ALL GOES WRONG

All of this goes wrong when people become addicted to pornography. Here are the essentials of what might happen for a fictional fifteen-year-old we'll call Eustus. Eustus is growing up in a Christian family. As he goes through puberty, he's flooded with sexual urges and desires. One day he gives in to the temptation to view pornography and clicks on one of those links his parents warned him about and tried to restrict. It opens to him a world of sexual excitement and fantasy that's like a powerful magnet drawing him in. He begins to masturbate to these images in a more and more habitual—even compulsive—way. The results:

1. *Isolation*: Eustus begins to pull back from other good pursuits out of shame and the desire to hide his behavior—and to give more time to the excitement of this fantasy world. He misses out on more and more chances to develop friendships with other boys and girls. He becomes more awkward with other people and is frustrated that he rarely seems to connect with anybody. He doesn't understand why he's so lonely. Most of his "friends" are people he doesn't really know personally: video game partners on the web or people with whom he swaps tips about where to find the hottest pornography.

2. *Highs and lows*: The flood of new and powerful images is almost overwhelming. Scientists say the effect of this on the brain is rather like the high caused by an injection of the purest form of heroin. Eustus can't resist masturbating to the images he sees. He feels guilty, but he finds himself going back to the pornography again and again. The more hooked he is on pornography, the more Eustus withdraws at school, at church, and in his family. His ability to build real relationships deteriorates. His few limited friendships don't bring him the pleasure they used to, because his brain responds even less to what used to be the pleasures of normal interactions and friendships.

3. *Craving for more*: Just like that of a drug addict, Eustus's brain struggles to adjust to its extreme responses to the raw power

of the pornography. As a result, to get the same high as before, he needs more extreme porn. He ventures into areas of pornography that contain more twisted and degrading images. He never imagined he would get sucked in so deep.

4. *Withdrawal*: Eustus begins to realize that his grades are suffering, and he is increasingly alone and lonely. He tries to stop, but because his brain is accustomed to a pattern, his cravings intensify and normal interactions with others fail to provide any relief or satisfaction. It almost feels painful not to use porn. And even minor stresses such as running late for school trigger extreme cravings for more pornography.

5. *Falling behind*: Because the adolescent brain is at its peak capacity to learn and adapt quickly by forming new neuron connections, Eustus's brain loses ground in his development of self-control and mature judgment. As a result, Eustus's addiction is more deeply rooted in his brain than it would be in an adult brain and will take longer to change or heal. Further, Eustus has learned deeply destructive patterns and attitudes that will complicate any future relationship with a girlfriend or spouse. These include instincts that sexual pleasure (a) is something that happens in isolation with him in total control rather than in intimate interaction in which he shares with and learns from his wife and (b) can be instantly turned on with a click rather than developed through romance and intimacy in marriage.

## CONCLUSION

Moses grew up as the son of Pharaoh, discovered he was Jewish, committed murder in a futile effort to help his enslaved people, and ran away to build a life. God called him back to Egypt, where he miraculously led his people to freedom from the Egyptians. Their call was to go to their Promised Land. God parted the Red Sea, and Moses led them through, and then he watched the Egyptian army drown behind them.

Their plan to move immediately into the Promised Land was ruined by the disobedience and faithlessness of the people. They spent forty years wandering in the wilderness. Moses—and, more importantly, God—watched them waver between faithfulness to God and outright disobedience. Finally, as Moses neared the end of his life, it was time for his people to go to their Promised Land.

Through Moses, God made an impassioned plea. In essence, he said, "You are at a fork in the road: One route is marked *life* and the other *death*. Make the right choice." Read the passage for yourself; it is impassioned, sincere, clear, and decisive. God makes it clear that he doesn't expect the impossible and that he will help.

> For this commandment that I command you today is not too hard for you, neither is it far off. It is not in heaven. . . . Neither is it beyond the sea. . . . But the word is very near you. It is in your mouth and in your heart, so that you can do it.
>
> See, I have set before you today life and good, death and evil. If you obey the commandments of the LORD your God that I command you today, by loving the LORD your God, by walking in his ways, and by keeping his commandments and his statutes and his rules, then you shall live and multiply, and the LORD your God will bless you in the land that you are entering to take possession of it. But if your heart turns away . . . you shall surely perish. I call heaven and earth to witness against you today, that I have set before you life and death, blessing and curse. *Therefore choose life*, that you and your offspring may live, loving the LORD your God, obeying his voice and holding fast to him, for he is your life and length of days.
>
> DEUTERONOMY 30:11-20, EDITED AND EMPHASIS ADDED

As you make choices about sexual morality, you're making choices for life and death in every area. We chose this powerful passage for this chapter not because your decisions about pornography are bigger or more important than other areas of sexual morality—we chose it because there are very few areas where the choice between the way of life and the way of death is so clear.

When you choose life, you have a path that holds out the best promise for life with a faithful marriage partner with whom you can have a lifetime of love and sexual fulfillment. You can build a family and learn new depths of what it means to love and give. This path is outlined in God's law, and science repeatedly finds that people on this path experience the best outcomes in terms of satisfaction with life, relationships, and sex.

The way of death is a path to isolation, addiction, and soul-crushing loneliness. It's a life lived in a fantasy world that produces immediate gratification but robs you of everything that really matters in life.

How could the choice be clearer? As Moses urged his people, we also urge you to choose life. Protect your mind and heart by staying away from pornography. If you have begun to dabble in porn or, worse, if you're an actual user, we urge you to consult with a parent, a youth pastor or other staff member at your church, or a trusted adult.

## CHAPTER 16

# *Same-Sex Love*

**TEENAGERS EXPERIENCE** a complicated swirl of sexual feelings, but most of our readers will experience attraction to the other sex almost exclusively: men toward women and women toward men. Some of you will experience a confusing mixture of attraction to both men and women, and a few will mostly experience attraction to the same sex.

All the other chapters in this book that deal with romantic relationships are written with the assumption that readers are in the first category: heterosexual (or "straight"). We did that deliberately, because that's what most people experience, and we tried to address the needs of the majority.

This chapter is written, however, for teenagers who are discovering that they feel largely attracted to people of the same sex and feel very little attraction to people of the other sex. We hope all of our readers will read on to better understand how God would have us all respond to same-sex attraction.

If you consistently experience attractions to people of the same sex as you, making sense of what you feel and who you are is complicated—it's possibly deeply perplexing or even extraordinarily painful. The gap between public attitudes and what we hear in some of our churches can make it even harder.

In the United States a majority of people have come to accept LGBTQ persons (lesbian, gay, bisexual, transgender, questioning/queer) and their lifestyles just as they are. An even bigger majority in Canada and Western Europe have done the same. Many of you attend schools where full acceptance of LGBTQ persons is the norm and even the requirement. People who do not give such approval often are shamed and branded homophobic, noninclusive "haters," especially on social media.

In some traditional Christian churches, young people are presented an opposite view: that being gay is a choice and is an "abomination to the Lord," that such persons could change their orientation if they would just choose to repent, and that "those people" are our enemies in a colossal "culture war." Sadly, in some cases there's a hint of smug pride and judgment in how some Christian leaders talk about same-sex relationships.

In some very sad situations, young people have heard hateful and spiteful comments about gays and lesbians (or the harsh labels that are sometimes given to them) from church members, pastors, and even those within their peer groups or families. If this is happening or has happened to you, your growing awareness of your sexual feelings may be cause for terror, depression, and even questioning whether your life is going to be worth living.

We want to start by saying that God loves you regardless of the sexual feelings you have. God wants to guide you and walk with you down a path of life that's worth living—a path on which you can experience much love and joy.

How are you to make sense of all this? As has been our consistent pattern in this book, we begin with what the Bible teaches.

## WHAT DOES THE BIBLE TEACH ABOUT HOMOSEXUAL RELATIONSHIPS?

The Bible has much more to say about heterosexual sin in all its varieties than it does about the sins of gay people. But it's not silent on this topic.

Despite forceful claims to the contrary, sexual intercourse between two people of the same sex is never praised and is strongly condemned in every place it's mentioned in the Scriptures. The clearest passages are the four on these pages: two from the Old Testament and two from the New Testament.

> You shall not lie with a male as with a woman; it is an abomination.
>
> LEVITICUS 18:22

> If a man lies with a male as with a woman, both of them have committed an abomination.
>
> LEVITICUS 20:13

> Do you not know that the unrighteous will not inherit the kingdom of God? Do not be deceived: neither the sexually immoral, nor idolaters, nor adulterers, nor men who practice homosexuality, nor thieves . . . will inherit the kingdom of God. And such were some of you. But you were washed, you were sanctified, you were justified in the name of the Lord Jesus Christ and by the Spirit of our God.
>
> 1 CORINTHIANS 6:9-11

> For this reason God gave them up to dishonorable passions. For their women exchanged natural relations for those that are contrary to nature; and the men likewise gave up natural relations with women and were consumed with passion for one another, men committing shameless acts

> with men and receiving in themselves the due penalty for their error.
>
> ROMANS 1:26-27

Much could be and has been said about these verses, but we will cut to the core of what they say and what they don't say.

These verses say clearly that God does not approve of sexual intercourse between people of the same sex. Further, the Romans passage tells us that the desire for same-sex intercourse or intimacy isn't what God designed us to experience (it's "unnatural," which means it's a result of sin and brokenness). The Corinthians passage clarifies that people who once practiced such things can repent (turn away from former sinful behavior) and be washed, forgiven, sanctified, and justified so that they're in full fellowship with Christ.

What do these verses *not* say? They don't say that God despises same-sex sinners, nor do they say it's ever right for any Christian to despise them. They don't say that same-sex intercourse is unforgivable. Rather, the sin of homosexual sex is just one of many ways in which people disobey God and need to be rescued by him. And these verses don't promise that all same-sex attractions can be converted to attractions to the other sex.

How, then, can some people claim the Bible teaches acceptance of same-sex love?

## WHAT WOULD JESUS DO?

Some argue that Jesus is the champion of the outcasts and rejects from mainstream society and, therefore, that he loves and accepts LGBTQ persons exactly as they are, including accepting any loving behavior consistent with the desires of their hearts. This is a flawed argument. Jesus indeed loves the outcasts exactly as they are, but he doesn't accept their sins—he calls sinners to forsake their sinful lives and follow him, just as he did with the woman caught in adultery in John 8:11 (Jesus said, "Go, and from now on sin no more"), the tax collector Zacchaeus in Luke 19, and the Samaritan woman in John 4.

Some argue that since there's no record in the Gospels of Jesus directly saying anything about same-sex relationships, we can conclude he has no problem with such relationships. This is a bad argument for three reasons: First, while Jesus challenged religious practices that were based on misinterpretations of Old Testament laws, he said clearly that he came not to "abolish the Law or the Prophets . . . but to fulfill them" (Matthew 5:17). Second, on those few occasions in Jesus' ministry when he talked about sexual morality, he always tightened rather than loosened the law. He went beyond adultery to condemn lust (Matthew 5:27-30), and when he talked about divorce (see Matthew 19:1-12), he tightened the bonds of marriage compared to the practice of the time. Third, if you believe that having no direct statement from Jesus on a certain behavior means it's okay, what about his silence on rape or incest?

## OTHER COMMON ARGUMENTS

Individuals who oppose biblical truth have written thousands and thousands of pages arguing that the Bible approves of same-sex relationships, often using the following kinds of arguments:

- "Paul used Greek words with unknown or unusual meanings."
- "What Paul condemned was only specific kinds of same-sex acts, such as gay prostitution, adult abuse of children or youth who were slaves, or sexual acts performed with pagan priests. Modern same-sex love was unknown in the ancient world and never discussed."
- "The highest ethical principle is love, and love for LGBTQ people overrules condemnation, making these biblical passages irrelevant."

Prominent scholars, however, have discredited all such arguments. Paul's language clearly includes all gay sex. Archaeologists and historians have documented awareness of homosexual orientation in the ancient Roman world. As a result, it's clear that the Bible's condemnations of same-sex love include consensual adult relationships rather than just abusive relationships. And God's commandments not to sin are an expression of his love—not the opposite.

There are quite a number of scholars and theologians who simply say the Bible is wrong. For instance, a well-known New Testament scholar admits that the Bible condemns same-sex relationships. He said, "I think it important to state clearly that we do, in fact, reject the straightforward commands of Scripture."[1] He calls on biblical scholars to stop their efforts to twist the Bible to say that it approves of same-sex love.

Rejection of these clear commands in the Bible is spiritually disastrous. Jesus says that if we love him, we will do as he commands. It's okay to question whether we have interpreted the Bible correctly, but it's spiritually disloyal to "reject the straightforward commands of Scripture." To do that is to put our judgments above those of God and his inspired Word—this is rebellion against God.

> [Jesus said,] "If anyone loves me, he will keep my word, and my Father will love him, and we will come to him and make our home with him. Whoever does not love me does not keep my words."
>
> JOHN 14:23-24

We must conclude that the Bible—God's Word—condemns sexual intercourse between two people of the same sex. And all sexual intercourse outside the bonds of marriage between a man and woman is contrary to God's will.

As we say this, however, we want to make one important clarification:

Full same-sex intimacy is sinful, but feelings of attraction to people of the same sex are not sinful. The strong words of Romans 1 tell us that the origins or causes of same-sex attractions lie in the broken state of our world (here *world* means "everything," including our own bodies, minds, and souls—all of which have been damaged by sin). A desire to do what is sinful is not in itself wrong. A desire to have sex with someone you're attracted to is natural—it's acting upon it by either doing it or taking steps toward doing it that would be wrong.

Christ calls us to follow him with radical devotion, putting him first in all things. We are to hear and obey God's Word and will as revealed in the Scriptures.

## BUT ARE THERE NEW FACTS THAT CHALLENGE US?

For three thousand years or more, the Christian church and the faithful believers of the Old Testament before them consistently have taught that same-sex intimacy is inappropriate. Has new knowledge arisen that should shake our confidence in this biblical teaching? Have we learned anything that should convince us that we have misinterpreted Scripture?

Looking at the reasoning behind the 2015 United States Supreme Court majority decision legalizing same-sex marriage (it passed five votes to four) can help us briefly lay out what some consider to be such new facts. Considering these is important for thinking about this issue in general, but it can be critical for young people who are experiencing these feelings and trying to decide what to do with them and where to turn.

### Presumed Fact #1: *Gay and bisexual people, like heterosexuals, are born that way.*

Some believers have accepted the following mistaken argument: "Science has proved that we're all born with our sexual orientation 'wired in,' determined by our genes. If gay people are born that way, God made them that way and accepts them as they are, so we should too."

Science, however, has *not* proved that we're born with predetermined sexual orientations. If homosexual orientation is caused by our genes, then identical twins (two people born with identical genes) should always match for sexual orientation. What does the evidence show?

A study examined all identical twins born in Sweden over a number of decades, with scientists examining how often both identical twins were gay.[2] In the vast majority of the thousands of identical twin pairs, both twins were straight, but they found seventy-one male identical twin pairs in which at least one of the two twin men was gay. Were all of the other twins in each pair (what scientists call the "co-twins") also gay? Far from it. In fact, the scientists found that of the seventy-one male identical twin pairs, in only seven cases was the second identical twin also gay. The vast majority of identical twin pairs did not match for homosexual orientation. The scientific evidence thus suggests that genetics is a minor contributing cause to sexual orientation.

So what causes sexual orientation? At this point, the causes are still a scientific mystery. Genetics may contribute in a minor to moderate way, as may other biological factors. So also may subtle or blatant experiences children have in their families, neighborhoods, schools, or other settings, including abusive parents, sexual abuse, and many other possibilities.

But does the cause of orientation matter to the question of right or wrong? No. Christian faith teaches that we're all subject to sinful desires and brokenness we didn't choose. We're all born with sin natures. We didn't choose this—Adam and Eve made that choice when they rebelled against God. Their choice ruined not just our internal nature but also the world around us—their sin introduced disease, brokenness, and all kinds of twistedness into the world.

As a result, some of us are born with or develop inclinations toward alcoholism, drug addiction, violence, and other forms of human brokenness. Some give in to such inclinations, and some choose otherwise. God allows such inclinations, but sin is the cause, not God. And some born without such inclinations make bad choices anyway. Inclinations or not, all of us are accountable for our choices.

**Presumed Fact #2:** ***Sexual orientation cannot be changed.***

There is conclusive scientific evidence that some people *do* experience change in their sexual orientation. Some lesbians (gay women) demonstrate a degree of what's called "sexual fluidity." Our own research has shown that some men and women report change in their sexual orientation through participation in religiously oriented change attempts.[3] The percentage of people that change is small, but it doesn't appear to be impossible for some.

But more important, this is what the Bible teaches: The apostle Paul, after declaring that people who practice wickedness—including same-sex intimacy—cannot inherit the kingdom of God, immediately declared, "Such were some of you." He was talking about people who had changed somehow.

That change doesn't mean complete conversion from gay to straight, however. Paul could be talking about people who left immorality behind and embraced chastity despite continuing to be attracted to the same sex. You don't need to have sex to have a beautiful and rich life in Christ. Jesus lived a life of complete chastity. Our churches need to do a better job of supporting individuals who have such a lifestyle.

**Presumed Fact #3:** ***Marriage is a creation of human culture; its nature can change (and has changed) over time.***

Marriage may be and has been changed by human action. But the truth remains that God created marriage as one of his greatest gifts to humanity. That it can be changed by human choices (such as the act of divorce) doesn't mean it should be. This is why so many Christians objected to the 2015 Supreme Court redefinition of marriage. We may distort marriage by our actions, but the imprint of God's original design will never be changed.

**Presumed Fact #4:** ***Each individual has the right to express (to live out) his or her sexual identity.***

From a legal perspective, the four Supreme Court judges who voted against legalizing gay marriage argued that the majority badly twisted the clear meaning of the US Constitution to find in those words written long ago a "right to express sexual identity." But whether or not there's such a constitutional or governmental right, from a Christian perspective our obligation is to live as followers of Jesus Christ. We give up our rights to God, believing that his will is for our ultimate blessing. Our right and obligation to follow him is our most precious right.

**Presumed Fact #5:** ***Objections to Presumed Facts #1–4 are based not in rational thought but in fear, ignorance, disapproval, or even hatred of gay people.***

People who question Presumed Facts 1 through 4 are often dismissed as "haters." There *are* people who detest gay people and whose objections to gay marriage are rooted in hatred and homophobia. But here we have responded without hatred and without fear of gay people. We simply feel these presumed facts are wrong.

## WHY IS SAME-SEX LOVE WRONG?

We believe that the biblical teaching is that same-sex intimacy—just like sex outside of the bounds of marriage between one woman and one man—is contrary to the will of God. But why would God regard the actions of LGBTQ people as unacceptable? Why would he not want them to experience pleasure or express love sexually to enrich and fulfill their lives?

People today are bombarded with messages that there's no higher purpose than pleasure or personal happiness. The Christian faith says the opposite: Our world and our lives are infused with spiritual meaning and purpose. As we argued in chapter 3, the first purpose of people is to reflect God's image.

In Ephesians, the apostle Paul said that when he spoke about marriage, he was really speaking about Christ and his bride, the church. God's eternal purposes from Creation onward were for human beings as individuals, families, and communities to manifest God's image, to be his representatives, to be windows through which the world would see his character.

Included in this is the idea that marriage between one each of two basic types of human beings—a man and a woman—would be a union where the two become one while still remaining individuals. In a way that no other relationship can, this reflects the unity yet individual identities within the Trinity. When marriage results in children, that marriage reflects the way that the individuality and unity between and among the Father, Son, and Holy Spirit overflow in loving creativity and goodness to create humanity made in the image of God. A monogamous traditional marriage demonstrates to the world the exclusive and covenantal love of God.

Marriage and family, though, isn't the only way to image God. Chaste (sexually pure) single persons in community follow the path of Jesus' own life and equally reflect to the watching world the faithful, loyal, and self-giving character of God. Both marriage and chastity are life patterns of dignity and blessing.

### "I HAVE TO BE ME!"

But what about the way LGBTQ people see their sexuality as key to their identities? Time and time again you will face the fundamental question *What is the core of my identity?* The message that comes from the world today is that you should embrace your sexual orientation as the core of your identity: "Who are you? You're gay—end of discussion."

We believe the Christian faith calls us to a different answer. The calling to be a disciple of Christ is a calling to radical obedience—it's a call not to embrace what we are but to become what we are not. Christ calls us to give up everything for him. On what basis will you form your identity? What did God make us to be? We're called to become like Christ, and that calls us on a journey of self-sacrifice. Our sexual feelings cannot and should not define us. Above all else we're God's beloved sons and daughters.

## SO WHAT DOES THIS MEAN FOR YOU?

This is an urgent personal issue for those who feel some sort of attraction toward people of the same sex. There's a common myth that everyone falls cleanly and perfectly from birth into one of two categories: straight or gay. This is often coupled with the belief that if you have any sexual feelings other than heterosexual feelings, you're gay. Neither is true.

The confusing thing is that many of us go through periods when our sexual feelings are mixed-up, uncertain, and troubling. Many boys feel strong sexual desire and have erections without any clear understanding of what has them excited. Many boys and girls have sexual dreams of hugging or kissing people without any clues as to who the people are—even if they're men or women. Girls often have such strong emotional feelings of love for their girlfriends that they wonder if those are sexual feelings.

As we go through puberty, we have a lot of curiosity about the bodies of the opposite sex but also about the bodies of people of the same sex. For instance, a boy might look around in a locker room to see how other boys are developing. He might wonder if his curiosity about other boys means he's gay. If he's caught looking around, other boys may tease him about it and call him gay.

Many of us experience mixed, complicated attractions to different people, and we're not defined by any one attraction. A boy may see a scene of sexual violence on TV—say of an attempted rape—and feel some sexual excitement. This doesn't mean that boy is a rapist. It's just a reminder that he has to work hard to make choices that will help him honor God. Another example might be people who have experienced some kind of sexual abuse that leaves them deeply confused about sexual attraction.

As our society moves to more acceptance of homosexual behavior, young adults will likely be more confused about whether their feelings point to a same-sex orientation. The problem is that same-sex attractions aren't something that only lifelong homosexual people have—heterosexual people can have them too, though they don't feel them as often or as strongly.

Our sexuality is complicated, especially since sin is part of every aspect of our lives, confusing us and leaving us torn by conflicting and evil desires. If you do have occasional homosexual feelings as you go through your teenage years, this generally is nothing to worry about. It's part of the normal range of feelings that go along with growing up.

The growing acceptance of LGBTQ lifestyles has led to more young adults experimenting with such behavior to see if that's their orientation. This is something you should avoid. Some people will directly ask, "How will you know whether you're gay unless you try it?" You shouldn't experiment in this way, but if you do, know that your behavior doesn't define your identity. We've known adults who aren't gay who were involved in homosexual practices while they were teenagers, sometimes with kids their own age, sometimes with slightly older kids, and sometimes with adults.

If you find these feelings are strong and consistent, and you don't have any feelings of attraction toward people of the opposite sex, then you may want to talk about it with someone you trust. We urge you to make choices that honor God by accepting his teaching that same-sex intimacy is wrong and by committing yourself to sexual purity. You need to flee from all forms of sexual immorality, and that includes same-sex behavior.

### A FINAL WORD TO EVERYONE

To those readers whose dominant attraction is toward the other sex, we emphasize your responsibility to love, care for, and support Christian peers whose experience is otherwise. Do so in exactly the way God does: by being completely loving, supportive, and loyal while remaining faithful to the true teachings of Scripture, including the teaching that sex between persons of the same sex is wrong.

We live in a time when many gay and lesbian people are fighting for complete acceptance by the church. Gay and lesbian support groups that aim to help young people discover and accept their feelings of same-sex attraction are becoming increasingly common; "gay pride" activities and organizations are active in many schools.

As we mentioned, the Supreme Court legalized same-sex marriage in 2015. Same-sex marriage is now the law of the land in the United States. Does this decision have moral authority over Christian believers? We believe it does not. The Supreme Court, with all nine justices in agreement, deliberately set aside all specifically religious arguments about the morality of gay marriage in making their decision—they had to do so because the US Constitution specifies government neutrality toward any religion.

But that's *not* our situation as individuals. To be Christians, we must believe that Jesus is our Lord. He's the supreme ruler of our lives no matter the countries in which we reside. We answer first to *him* and not to any court, president, king, parent, pastor, or anyone else.[4] He demands first place in our lives.

Because Jesus is our Lord, religious freedom is our responsibility and obligation and not just a right. We're to follow the example in

Acts 5 of Peter and the apostles. There, the apostles were arrested and thrown in prison for openly preaching the gospel in Jerusalem. An angel miraculously freed them, and they went right back to preaching the gospel.

The officials arrested them again, angrily demanding they stop, but "Peter and the apostles answered, 'We must obey God rather than men'" (Acts 5:29). That's religious freedom. We're free not because a government allows us to be free or grants us this right. No, we're free because God sets us free.

What will we do with our freedom? We must balance two difficult responsibilities: (1) to tell the truth and (2) to love with abandon. Some of our churches have done a terrible job of being loving places where people can understand their struggles, open their hearts to one another, and sincerely and transparently seek God. Our churches need to do a better job of humbly approaching sexuality issues, recognizing that we're all broken creatures.

Some of us lack the courage to tell the truth in love. Jesus Christ demonstrated the capacity to love and speak the truth at the same time. The Bible calls us to love, and it calls us to live by God's commandments. This is our call. Those of us who are seeking to be sincere Christ-followers and have feelings of attraction to people of the same sex deserve nothing less.

CHAPTER 17

# *Male OR Female? (or Other?)*

**FIFTY YEARS AGO,** "Are you male or female?" seemed a simple question. There were only two possible answers. If there was any doubt whether you were male or female, you likely were seen as having some kind of psychological confusion or problem.

Some of you have grown up in homes, schools, and churches that continue to see this as a simple question. Some, on the other hand, have grown up in homes, schools, and churches where the question isn't simple at all.

No matter how we view the question, for most of us the *personal* answer is simple: Most of us who have vaginas and other female anatomy feel comfortably like girls or women, and most of us with penises feel comfortably like boys or men. But for some, your personal answer is complicated because you do not feel as sure or comfortable.

## IT'S GETTING COMPLICATED

"Are you male or female?" is, in the minds of many today, too simple a question, or even the wrong question. "What is your preferred gender?" and "What gender best describes you?" are the questions many of you are more likely to be asked. Possible answers, it is argued, are not determined by your anatomy, and they aren't restricted just to two options: male or female. Literally dozens and dozens of other gender options, an ever-increasing number, are being proposed.[1]

It is important to note that this new view pushes aside our bodily realities and assumes or argues that it is our feelings, our gut intuitions, our total psychological experiences that rule everything. This shift is resulting in regulations or laws in some situations. For instance, there are new public school policies saying the sex of students (even students as young as three or four) isn't determined by what it says on their birth certificates, by their genitals, or by what their parents say. It's set by the child's personal "gender identity" and "gender expression."

*Gender identity* refers to a person's private, internal sense of their sex. Imagine a third grader named Julie who says, "I've never felt I was a girl; I've always sensed that I'm really a boy." *Gender expression* refers to how people show to others through their actions and choices their internal sense of sex; for instance, Julie shows up at school with short hair, wearing the type of clothes typical of boys, insisting on being treated as a boy, and referring to herself as *Judd*.

It's not just schools that are changing. Some parents choose to raise their children without assuming they're one sex or the other. They intend to leave the choice up to their children. There are transgender characters in many TV shows and movies, and popular music frequently celebrates the freedom of people to make these decisions for themselves.

All of this can be very confusing or unsettling as you're growing up.

## AND THEN WHAT HAPPENS?

In the past, and in some settings today, some struggled with the match between their sexual anatomy and their feelings and perceptions, but it was a private, hidden struggle. More people today believe that our bodies don't matter so much and that our feelings and self-perceptions—what we might call our internal experiences—are the real authority. Further, some young people are drawn to the community and shared identity of others like themselves. Some people are changing the way they live their lives as they embrace this way of thinking.

*Here's a small sample of the complicated and debated language about sex and gender:*

**Transgender** *is the most common term for someone whose sexual anatomy is clearly male or female, but who feels that their sense of gender does not line up with their anatomy. They may have a penis but feel more like a girl, or like a mixture of both, or neither.*

**Transsexuals** *are a specific type of transgender person whose sexual anatomy is clearly male or female, but who feels that their sense of gender closely matches the other sex. One example would be a biological male who intensely identifies as a woman (and who perhaps self-describes as "a woman trapped in a man's body"). Some reserve this term for those who take the additional step of seeking medical treatments to change their bodies.*

*Some object to the assumption that there are only two options for gender, male or female; they argue there are any number of identities between or beyond male or female. Male and female are not the only two (*__binary__*) choices; these people argue that* **gender nonbinary** *is a better label.*

*Many transgender persons and those supporting them resist using the word* **normal** *for those whose sexual anatomy and subjective sense of themselves match comfortably (for example, a kid with a penis who feels completely like a boy). They use the term* **cisgendered** *to refer to such persons; "cis" is Latin for "on this side" and is the opposite of "trans," which means "on the other side."*

For some, this involves pushing back against the customs and expectations of parents, church, society, or whatever (together, what are called "gender stereotypes and norms"). Some young men and women adopt dress, mannerisms, hairstyles, and other outward characteristics not typical for their sex. Others take it further and completely reject their identity as a boy or girl, choosing instead to live as if they were a person of the other sex or of their own defined gender (without the use of medical interventions).

But advances in medical science have opened up a whole new range of additional options. Today, those options include

- administering drugs to delay the onset of puberty for children questioning their gender and sex
- administering drugs to suppress the hormones produced by young adult bodies, and administering artificial hormones of the other sex to push the body toward the desired outcome, such as a woman becoming more masculine
- cosmetic interventions such as hair removal or stimulation of hair growth
- surgery to remove parts of the sexual anatomy that conflict with the person's subjective gender identity
- surgery to construct artificial sexual anatomy that aligns with the person's gender identity

When a person who is questioning their gender takes deliberate steps toward shaping their actions and even anatomy toward conformity with their gender identity, the person is said to be "transitioning." A step in transition can be as minor as cutting one's hair shorter or growing it longer, or it can be as radical as removing a penis and attempting to replace it through surgery with an artificial vagina.

## SO WHAT'S THE ANSWER?

We know people who have struggled with this question all their lives and have experienced great pain because of it. Some have even considered or attempted suicide. We want to write in a way that's respectful of those who have experienced such pain. The best way we know to be both respectful and loving is to write in a way that's faithful to God and his will for our lives.

Those who are blessed with a confident sense that their physical bodies align with their inner sense of identity should treat with love and respect our fellow human beings who experience a mismatch between the two. That doesn't mean supporting their every action or decision, but it does mean we should love them and so should the church.

The question "What's your preferred gender designation?" presumes two things: (1) that one's physical anatomy is a lower priority (if it's a priority at all) in determining our gender identity; and (2) that the categories of male and female aren't real and distinct things—or at least they're not the only two categories. We believe, however, that male and female are the only two categories that reflect God's purposes in creation, which ultimately makes them the only valid categories for us. Why? Because it was God's intent that there be two sexes, male and female, *not* that there be an array of sexes between those two.

## SOME CHALLENGING REALITIES

We cannot argue this, however, without grappling with some challenging counterevidence to the Christian belief that male and female are ultimately the two categories for sex that were intended by God from Creation.

First, if there are only two sexes, male and female, how do we understand the medical condition called *intersex* (what previously was referred to as *true hermaphroditism*)? People with this rare condition are, for a variety of reasons, born with mixed or blended testicular and ovarian tissues that produce both male and female hormones. As a result, they have ambiguous genital anatomy: typically an underdeveloped, partial vagina and an overdeveloped clitoris (or small penis) without a urinary opening at the end. Their other sex characteristics are mixed too. Thus, they defy our hard categories of male and female.

This rare condition occurs in less than one in two thousand babies born. There are a variety of other rare physical conditions that also complicate determining whether a specific child with that condition is physically a male or female. Combining these with intersex condition persons, chances are probably less than one in one thousand that a child will have such a condition.

Second, there is no single factor that defines a typical male or female. A "normal" female, for instance, has a vagina and all of the other external genital structures, *plus* a uterus, ovaries, and the other internal structures, *plus* normal levels of estrogen and the other female hormones, *plus* enlarged breasts and the other secondary sex characteristics, *plus* brain structures and connections typical of the average female, *plus* she identifies as a female (gender identity), *plus* she acts like a female (gender expression), *plus* she is sexually attracted to men (sexual orientation).

With this many factors determining sex and gender, what happens when those factors do not all point in the same direction? The passionate argument of the community of people who call themselves various versions of *transgender* is that when people consistently, deeply, and sincerely experience gender identities that don't line up with their physical characteristics, it's their identities and their experiences that take priority. Some might say they're men trapped in women's bodies (or the reverse); others say their gender identities are more fluid, and so forth. They argue that the depth of these feelings demands that we accept their experiences as legitimate and recognize them as something other than male and female.

## BUT MALE AND FEMALE ARE REAL!

There are three basic arguments in response: First, humanity has almost universally recognized the distinction of male and female as fundamental throughout its history and has seen the union of one of each as the core requirement of marriage and family. The reality is that the creation of a new life, a baby, requires one man and one woman to come together sexually. The fact that each contributes something distinct to the creation of a new life signals that there are two types of human beings, male and female.

Second, the fact that "exceptions" such as intersex exist—as has been noted historically and even more today—does not change the fundamental point. We must ask whether these exceptions mean that we need to add other categories of sexes, or instead whether we should see such cases as exceptions to the basic, valid categories. We may truly say that dogs have four legs and a tail, but when we see a three-legged, tailless dog, we still see it as a dog despite the fact that it breaks the rule. Similarly, a woman who has her ovaries removed to prevent cancer doesn't cease to be a woman. The same holds for the loss of two characteristics contributing to the designation of sex (ovaries and uterus) and even three (ovaries, uterus, and breasts).

That leads us to our third point. Advocates may argue that someone who grows up with the firmly rooted sense that their identity is at odds with their body is totally different from a woman who grew up with an identity firmly rooted as a woman who then has her uterus, ovaries, and breasts removed. But Christians believe three fundamental and important things that guide our response in such cases:

- We believe that God intended for humans to be either male or female. "So God created man [meaning all of humanity] in his own image, in the image of God he created him; male and female he created them" (Genesis 1:27). We discussed the significance of this in chapters 2 and 3.
- We believe that God intentionally made us physical, bodily beings, and that our bodies matter. They are, in fact, a gift from God.

- Finally, we also believe the Bible tells us why things go wrong and confusing exceptions occur: It's because humanity rebelled against God. Sin has twisted and broken everything: our hearts, minds, bodies, and world. Nothing about our world or us is "normal," the "normal" God intended. Sin has twisted and broken everyone; we are all twisted and all fail to be what God wants us to be. Those who do not struggle with gender identity can't be the proud "normal" ones pointing fingers. We have to be humble ones who say, "I'm so blind and broken I can only know what is right and good, and what's not, by the light of the Bible, God's Word."

It's hard to understand why some people don't identify with or experience themselves as the sex of their physical bodies—for instance, the person with a female body who doesn't have a female gender identity. Christians will approach such persons believing that male and female are real, enduring categories, categories for which there are tragic complications and confusions because of the brokenness of the world. This leads us to see gender identities other than male and female as reflections of our shared human brokenness and not as true and good alternative gender identities. Based on these and other important theological concerns, we approach the area of gender identity misalignment with compassion, concern, and caution.

## WRAPPING UP

There's so much more that could be said. You face a daunting world. People whose gender identity differs from their physical sex are our fellow human beings. They, too, are made in the image of God. They should be treated with love and respect. But at the same time, we humbly say that male and female are fundamental categories of human existence. We believe further that something has gone wrong when a person of one biological sex identifies as some other designation. We can and must show compassion when that happens.

If you're a person who experiences conflict between your physical sex and your identity, we urge you to prayerfully submit this to God as a departure from God's creational intent. It's important to realize that your departure starts with things *you did not choose*: your genes and your less-than-perfect experiences in your family and social world. No one asks for such mixed-up feelings.

But at the same time, God has given humans the capacity to make choices, some big and some small. Know that God loves you. We urge you over the long term to choose to bring such feelings to God for his comfort, his insight, and as much healing as he grants. Do so with people who love you and who are mature in Christian faith.

We also ask you to consider the fact that all of the major mental health and medical organizations call for extreme caution in considering the use of powerful drugs or irreversible surgery in response to confusion about gender identity. They call for caution because such interventions are truly dramatic steps to take.

These organizations also call for caution because there are so many ways in which unhappiness and distress, emotional conflict and suffering, can be mistakenly understood as being just a symptom of a problem with one's gender identity. In some communities, there is even pressure from peers and advocates that being straight or cisgendered is biased and boring, while questioning one's gender identity is socially praised and provides an enthusiastic base of unwavering support.

There are some young people and adults who began the transition process, even to the point of having surgery, who later recognized their gender identity was not the real source of their unhappiness. It was something else entirely. There are quite a number of voices who say something like "I thought my problems came from being a man in a woman's body, but I later discovered that I was a woman who struggled with severe anxiety about being with others as a woman. I had many questions about what that meant for me."

If your physical body doesn't align with your inner sense of identity, we empathize with your pain. We apologize and ask your forgiveness for any actions that have added to the pain you feel. Because we love you and because you matter to us and to God, we must tell you that our Christian faith leads us to believe your experience is not something to celebrate but rather to regard as a kind of departure from God's original plan, a kind of brokenness. It's something for which to seek comfort from God's presence, counsel, growth, and grace. We urge you prayerfully to seek out wise Christians with whom to pray and seek God's direction for your life.[2]

## CHAPTER 18

# *Other Questions and Tough Challenges*

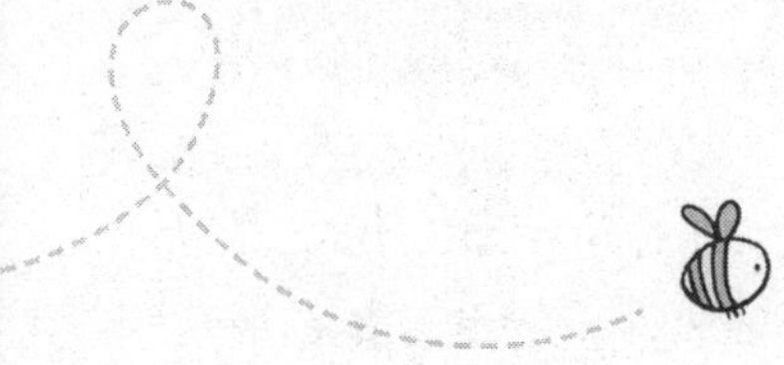

**WE HAVE SAID** so much in this book—and still there's much more that could be said. In this chapter we offer brief answers to some frequently raised issues and make suggestions about special challenges we have not yet addressed.

### WHAT IF MY PARENTS DIDN'T HANDLE THEIR SEXUALITY IN THE RIGHT WAY?

The most frequent reason parents give for feeling uncomfortable about talking with their kids about sex is that they're not proud of how they handled their sexuality before they got married.

Parents might be nervous that their children could ask, "Mom and Dad, did you have sex or live together before you got married?" Parents might worry that giving honest answers may seem like giving permission to children to behave as they did. Parents want their children to make better choices than they did. Yet they don't want to lie to their children, so many parents avoid the subject of sex in hopes that their own pasts won't come up.

What if your mom or dad made choices in the past that they're not proud of? The truth is, you don't need to repeat your parents' past mistakes. In fact, you have the opportunity to make better decisions than they did and so experience more of the joy and blessing of God's gift of sexuality. As parents talk to their children about their lives, their hope is that their children will see their weaknesses but not use those weaknesses as excuses to have the same ones. Parents hope each one of their children will make better decisions than they have and live better lives than they did. Nothing could make parents happier.

If your parents are willing to talk about their pasts, talk with them. We tell parents not to explain to their kids any of the details of their sexual pasts but to talk with their kids about how they feel about it now that they have grown as Christians. Most Christian parents who have broken God's rules about sex are able to tell their kids about the pain, suffering, and difficulty caused by their choices.

### PUBLIC SCHOOL SEX EDUCATION

You can learn many useful things in public school sex-education classes. These classes can give you good information about the biological aspects of sex, including more information about your body than we've covered in this book. Sex-education classes can also be opportunities to find out what your peers think about sex.

But sex-education classes also can be very discouraging to Christian teenagers. Some teachers assume that most of the kids in the class will be having sex. They may say once or twice that it's good not to have sex before marriage, but then the rest of the time might be spent in a way that assumes all the kids in the class will be having sex. They may only discuss how to prevent pregnancy and disease when you do have sex. Discussions like that can leave you feeling as if you're the only one who has decided to save sex for marriage.

When you feel such discouragement, talk to your parents, your youth leader at your church, or respected adults or older Christian peers that can help you get perspective on the discussion. People who follow God have always struggled with being dismissed and made fun of by the people around them. You must be strong and brave and not rely on the approval of others to validate your beliefs.

Also, discussions about reasons for not having sex can be a problem. Some teachers and students don't respect Christian beliefs. In a sex-education class, Justin expressed his belief that God wants sex to be saved for marriage. Instead of this belief being accepted and encouraged, he was attacked for being "bossy" and "judgmental" for saying something that made other people feel guilty.

Sometimes when a teenager expresses a belief about God's view of sex, a teacher turns that view around and makes it appear that the real reason the teen chooses not to have sex is because of fear of sex or a negative view about it. Teens sometimes hear something like this: "It sounds as if you're really afraid of sex. Maybe your family taught that sex is a bad, dirty, and disgusting thing. But many people don't think it is. Why do you have such negative views of sex?" It can be very upsetting to be put on the spot like this in front of classmates.

You must recognize these tactics for what they are: attempts to intimidate and embarrass you to push you toward changing your beliefs. It may not be possible to directly confront your teacher about such tactics, but again, talk it over with a mature fellow believer.

Sometimes in discussions about different moral positions, Christian kids are asked to role-play as if they believe the opposite of their own views. Teachers will say this is to help you think through all the options before you make up your mind. But it's risky to even pretend that you believe sex outside marriage is okay. It's good for us to think through what we believe and to compare it to other beliefs, but God doesn't tell us to pretend to have other beliefs. God wants us to remain faithful to him at all times. You may need to tell a teacher that you don't feel you should have to defend a view you don't believe in.

Many public school sex-education programs focus on teaching kids how to use birth control, especially condoms and birth control pills. We've even heard of teens in eighth or ninth grade being required to go to stores to buy condoms. The reason given for this exercise is that it will help kids get over their embarrassment about using birth control.

There are several problems with this focus on birth control. First, the general attitude of the class that "all teenage kids are going to have sex, and here's how you can do it safely" is discouraging to Christian teenagers who have decided not to have sex. The second problem, as we discussed earlier, is that condoms and birth control pills are not perfectly safe. The kind of safety God wants for you comes from not having sex at all until you're married.

We pray that you will choose to save sex for marriage. But some teens, even those who grow up in Christian families, make wrong choices and have sex outside of marriage. When they do, they hurt themselves and they hurt God. If you choose not to follow God's way but instead have sex outside of marriage, then we urge you to use birth control. We don't urge you to do this because sex outside of marriage is okay. It isn't—sex outside of marriage is wrong in God's eyes. We urge you to do this because when you choose to have sex, you gamble with your life *and with other people's lives.* You can have a disease passed to you and then pass the disease to another person. You can get pregnant or get your partner pregnant. By using birth control, you're not making what you do less sinful. But you may reduce the amount of damage you do to others.

## BROKEN FAMILIES

Many Christian kids grow up in homes that have been shattered by divorce, separation, or death. You may live in a family in which there's only one parent or in a blended family created by a second or third marriage. Kids suffer a lot when their families break up; they often blame themselves for the breakups or feel responsibility to get their mothers and fathers back together. Kids feel lonely for the parents who aren't there. Kids in blended families face many problems, such as how to develop positive feelings for the strangers who are now their stepparents and how to get close to siblings they don't know well.

Living in a broken family can make it hard for a young person to think correctly about sex. Kids often do best when they have parents of both sexes present to talk to. It's important for girls to be able to understand men's perspectives on sexuality, and it's natural for girls to talk to their fathers about this. Similarly, boys can benefit from talking to their moms about women's perspectives. But if either your mom or your dad isn't available, you can ask the parent you live with who would be a good person for you to talk to.

What if your feelings about marriage have been soured by seeing your parents go through a messy divorce? Some of you may be thinking, *Well, I'm a Christian, and I'll follow God's rules about sex, but I don't ever plan to be married because I know how awful that can be.* Sadly, many marriages are painful. But marriage is still a gift from God, and when a marriage is good, it's a tremendous blessing. Don't give up on marriage, but do realize that every marriage involves struggle and sacrifice. For those of us who have good marriages, the joy and blessing we receive are well worth any struggle or sacrifice. Look around for Christian marriages that represent the goodness that God intends in marriage. These marriages can be a sign to you of the good that's possible.

If you live in a single-parent family where your parent is so tired from working that he or she doesn't have much energy left over to talk with you or go to your school activities, this can leave you feeling very alone. Talk with your parent about what might be done. It can help to develop Christian friendships through your church or school that can help you stay strong and make the right decisions. You may even be able to get close to the parents of some of your friends.

## SEXUAL ABUSE IN FAMILIES

This is a terribly sad topic to have to bring up. People have twisted and misused God's marvelous gift of sex in many ways, but perhaps none is as distressing as sexual abuse inside families. Sexual abuse inside a family is called *incest.* The most common form of sexual abuse within families is when an older brother forces his younger sister to do things for his sexual pleasure. Caitlyn grew up in a Christian family, but she was only ten years old when her fourteen-year-old brother began making her have sex with him. But not all sexual abuse involves sexual intercourse. An older brother might make his younger sister touch his genitals, or he may touch her genitals and get pleasure from it.

Sexual abuse also occurs when fathers, stepfathers, uncles, or cousins force sexual attention on children. Such force can come in the form of threatened or actual violence, but it can also come in the form of emotional or psychological manipulation. As with the above example, the resulting abuse could be sexual intercourse but could also be touching or other experiences. Though most sexual abuse happens to girls, boys can be sexually abused too, sometimes by women in their families but most often by men. Kevin was twelve when his older brother began making him do sexual things with him. All of this is terribly evil.

We pray this has never happened or will ever happen to you. Kids, especially girls, who experience sexual abuse in their families often feel they have no one they can turn to, no one who can help them escape these awful situations. If you have a friend who confides in you that he or she is being abused, you should definitely talk to your parents or to a trusted adult to get advice on how to stop it.

If you have been abused, take immediate steps to protect yourself and make the abuse stop. First, talk to your parents, particularly your mother. Mothers sometimes have a hard time believing such a thing is happening in their families, so you need to be prepared to calmly describe what has happened and to insist that you're not making it up. If for some reason you can't talk to a parent—or if your parent will not listen to you—then talk to your doctor, your pastor, or a school counselor. These people are required by law to take steps to protect you. The top priority is for you to be safe. God doesn't want you to be abused. And don't stay silent to try to keep your family together. The sad reality is abusers often abuse more than one victim. There's a good chance you're not the only victim, and so you need to stop the abuse.

After the abuse has stopped, it's important for you to get help for emotional healing. Healing of all the bad feelings and memories can be difficult, so it's very important you have someone you trust to talk with about this. Women who are sexually abused sometimes are repulsed by the idea of sex, hate and fear men, and have doubts about God. Sometimes children who have been sexually abused become very focused on sex and mistakenly think they have to act in sexual ways in order to be loved. Many young women who are abused feel horrible about themselves. They feel anger toward their own bodies, and they feel it must be their fault. But abuse is *not* their fault. If you have been abused and somebody has told you it was your fault, don't believe that person. Your body is not bad, sex is not bad, and not all men are bad. We urge you to talk to a very skilled pastoral counselor or Christian counselor, to pray to God, and to give yourself time to heal.

CHAPTER 19

# *What Kind of Person Should I Become?*

**YOU STAND AT** the very edge of young adulthood. For some of you, what we've been talking about seems far in the future. But many of you already know kids who are having sex, catching STIs, getting pregnant, having abortions, coming out as gay, changing genders, and so on.

As your body goes through the changes we described in this book, God is preparing you physically to be a mature sexual person. But becoming an adult is more than body changes.

Your parents have had a very strong influence on your life. Part of being a baby is being dependent on your parents for everything and being under their control and protection. As you go through elementary school, you begin the process of becoming independent from your parents. You develop more of a mind of your own as you spend time away from them and get a better sense of how other people look at things.

Over the next five to ten years, you'll become your own person. Growing up means making bigger and more important decisions. This can be, frankly, pretty scary—scary for you the teenager as you make decisions, and scary for your parents, who so badly want you to make the right decisions.

If you don't realize it already, it's time for you to understand a very important truth: *You're responsible for the kind of person you become.* Your decisions and choices determine what kind of person you are and will be. Your parents and friends will still have influence on you, but it's your decisions that will shape your life.

### "THE DEVIL MADE ME DO IT!"

Do you know people who talk as if they never make any choices? They don't say, "I did it because I thought that was the best thing to do" or "I did it because that's what I believed was right." Instead they say things like "He made me do it!" or "I had to do it, or my friends wouldn't like me anymore." This kind of thinking puts all the responsibility for choices on someone else.

But that doesn't change the truth that you are responsible for the kind of person you become. If you helped another kid cheat on a test because she begged you to, she didn't make you do it—you chose to do it because you wanted her to like you. If you watched a pornographic video so the guys would stop making fun of you, they didn't make you do it—you chose to do it because you didn't want them to make fun of you anymore.

You need to develop the habit of seeing how you're responsible for the decisions you make. Learn to think *I choose to do it* rather than *I have to do it.* Why? Because people who understand that they make the choices actually make better decisions.

## SMALL IS BIG

You must learn that you're responsible for what kind of person you become, and you must also learn that small choices are just as important as big ones. Kids who make bad decision after bad decision in the small areas tend later to make really big bad decisions when the pressure is on.

What seem like small, unimportant decisions make a difference in the area of sex as well. Whether or not you're a mature sexual person as an adult will depend on the kinds of small and big decisions you make over the next few years of your life. Deciding today whether you'll repeat or listen to dirty jokes, watch that pornographic movie at a friend's house, or connect to that sexual minority group on social media—these kinds of smaller decisions are as important as the big decisions you'll face later, because they all add together to make you who you are.

If the choices you make are so important, what can you do to help make the best choices? What are some good choices you can make now?

Most important, remember that nothing is more crucial than growing in your faith. Even as a young person, you need to decide whether you believe the truth of the Christian faith. You need to decide now who's going to be your number one commitment in life: you or God. And once you've decided to make God number one, having a mature faith is not something that just happens to you. It's something you work at all of your life. Faith is like a race, and the race is won by those who have the diligence and strength to keep going and to keep pressing on.

> I press on to make it my own, because Christ Jesus has made me his own. Brothers, I do not consider that I have made it my own. But one thing I do: forgetting what lies behind and straining forward to what lies ahead, I press on toward

> the goal for the prize of the upward call of God in Christ Jesus. Let those of us who are mature think this way, and if in anything you think otherwise, God will reveal that also to you.
>
> PHILIPPIANS 3:12-15

**GROWING WITH GOD**

So how do you keep going, and how do you grow in your faith?

One thing you can do is to make prayer an important part of your life. Prayer is asking things of God, but it's much more than that. Prayer is setting aside time to meet with God, to become quiet, and to allow God to speak to you. It's a time to be honest with God and ask him to point out what's good about your life and what needs changing. It's a time to ask God to forgive you for your wrong choices and actions and to thank him for forgiving you.

It's important to take some time every day by yourself (maybe in the morning or at night) to talk to God and listen to him as well. And you can pray short prayers all day about whatever's on your mind, such as "Lord, please help me to be strong and to forgive that bully who always picks on me in this class."

It's important to read the Bible. The Bible is God's Word. It is God speaking through human writers to tell us about himself. Someone once described the Bible as a collection of God's love letters to his children. If you don't have a version of the Bible written for someone your age, ask your parents to buy you one—if they can't do this, save up your money and buy a copy yourself. Ask a Christian bookstore worker which type of Bible is best for someone your age. There also are many free Bible apps for computers and mobile devices.

Read the Bible regularly and God will speak to you. Start with a book of the Bible such as John, Matthew, or Romans, and read a section or chapter each day. Think hard to figure out what it means; pray for God to speak to you.

It's hard to be a growing Christian on your own, so it's important that you attend a Bible-believing church where people are excited about their relationships with God. Participate in Bible studies and other activities. Get to know older Christian people who can teach you about growing up strong and true. Get to know a group of other Christian young people—nothing is more encouraging than having others around who believe the way you do.

Be obedient to God. The Bible says that when you don't obey God, your faith grows weak and dies. When you obey God, you get stronger. This book has been about how to obey God with your sexuality as you enter your teenage years. This is very important. But you need to obey God in all areas of your life, including your attitude, your relationship with your parents, and how you behave with your friends. Even those who try hard to obey will sometimes fail. When you fail, tell God what you have done; he will forgive you and make you stronger because you were honest with him (see 1 John 1:9).

> It is my prayer that your love may abound more and more, with knowledge and all discernment, so that you may approve what is excellent, and so be pure and blameless for the day of Christ, filled with the fruit of righteousness that comes through Jesus Christ, to the glory and praise of God.
>
> PHILIPPIANS 1:9-11

Finally, learn to pay close attention to the consequences of all your choices. Remember that as you become an adult, you need to take responsibility for what you choose to do and for the consequences of what you choose to do.

Welcome to the first stages of adulthood! Being an adult can be great, but how your life turns out rests mostly on your shoulders—on the decisions you make about how you will live your life. God wants to be right there with you to help as you make those decisions—he wants to give you his truth and strength and fill your heart with his love and forgiveness.

Sexuality is a wonderful part of God's design for your life, but it's up to you whether this gift will be a blessing or a curse. Our prayer for you is that you will use this gift as God intends and that you'll be able to celebrate with joy the blessings that flow from your sexuality.

# NOTES

**ACKNOWLEDGMENTS**

1. Stanton L. Jones, "How to Teach Sex: Seven Realities Christians in Every Congregation Need to Know," *Christianity Today* 55, no. 1 (January 2011): 34–39.

**CHAPTER 7: HOW DOES A WOMAN BECOME PREGNANT?**

1. For images and a detailed summary of male and female biological processes, please go to http://www.christiansexed.com/bringing-the-biology-together/.

**CHAPTER 9: FALSE ADVERTISING: A FAILED REVOLUTION**

1. Simon LeVay, Janice Baldwin, and John Baldwin, *Human Sexuality*, 4th ed. (New York: Oxford University Press, 2019), 185.
2. David Spiegelhalter, *Sex by Numbers: What Statistics Can Tell Us about Sexual Behaviour* (London: Profile Books, 2015).
3. Jean M. Twenge, Ryne A. Sherman, and Brooke E. Wells, "Declines in Sexual Frequency among American Adults, 1989–2014," *Archives of Sexual Behavior* 46, no. 8 (November 2017): 2389–2401.
4. Wendy Wang and Kim Parker, "Record Share of Americans Have Never Married: As Values, Economics and Gender Patterns Change," Pew Research Center, September 24, 2004: 4–5, 23, http://www.pewresearch.org/wp-content/uploads/sites/3/2014/09/2014-09-24_Never-Married-Americans.pdf.
5. Aaron Kheriaty, "Dying of Despair," *First Things* 275 (August–September 2017): 21–25.
6. Robert Putnam, *Bowling Alone: The Collapse and Revival of American Community* (New York: Simon & Schuster, 2000), 138.
7. Eric Klinenberg, quoted in Hannah Betts, "Being Single by Choice Is Liberating, Says Hannah Betts," *Telegraph*, March 21, 2013, https://www.telegraph.co.uk/women/womens-life/9930325/Being-single-by-choice-is-liberating-says-Hannah-Betts.html.
8. Jean M. Twenge, *Generation Me: Why Today's Young Americans Are More Confident, Assertive, Entitled—and More Miserable Than Ever Before* (New York: Atria, 2014).
9. Kheriaty, "Dying of Despair," 21–25.

10. Glynn Harrison, *A Better Story: God, Sex, and Human Flourishing* (London: InterVarsity Press UK, 2016), 105.
11. Sarah McLanahan and Isabel Sawhill, "Marriage and Child Wellbeing Revisited," *The Future of Children* 25, no. 2 (Fall 2015): 6, https://futureofchildren.princeton.edu/sites/futureofchildren/files/media/marriage_and_child_wellbeing_revisited_25_2_full_journal.pdf.
12. Harrison, *A Better Story*, 105.

**CHAPTER 16: SAME-SEX LOVE**

1. Luke Timothy Johnson, "Homosexuality and the Church: Scripture and Experience," *Commonweal* CXXXIV, no. 12 (June 15, 2007).
2. Niklas Långström et al., "Genetic and Environmental Effects on Same-Sex Sexual Behavior: A Population Study of Twins in Sweden," *Archives of Sexual Behavior* 39, no. 1 (February 2010): 75–80.
3. Stanton L. Jones and Mark A. Yarhouse, *Ex-Gays? A Longitudinal Study of Religiously Mediated Change in Sexual Orientation* (Downers Grove, IL: InterVarsity Press, 2007).
4. We must also recognize God does appoint and use these authorities in our lives—foremost godly and Christ-following parents—to teach and lead us into mature adulthood. In disagreements with parents, teachers, and others, you should be very sure that your read of God's direction is clear and right when it clashes with theirs. To claim "But Mom, God told me to have sex with my boyfriend" simply is a delusion.

**CHAPTER 17: MALE OR FEMALE? (OR OTHER?)**

1. One social media platform recently offered more than fifty possibilities with the option to write in new possibilities, creating an infinite number of possible choices. The specific choices offered were agender, androgyne, androgynous, bigender, cis, cisgender, cis female, cis male, cis man, cis woman, cisgender female, cisgender male, cisgender man, cisgender woman, female to male, FTM, gender fluid, gender nonconforming, gender questioning, gender variant, genderqueer, intersex, male to female, MTF, neither, neutrois, non-binary, other, pangender, trans, trans*, trans female, trans* female, trans male, trans* male, trans man, trans* man, trans person, trans* person, trans woman, trans* woman, transfeminine, transgender, transgender female, transgender male, transgender man, transgender person, transgender woman, transmasculine, transsexual, transsexual female, transsexual male, transsexual man, transsexual person, transsexual woman, and two-spirit.
2. Dr. Mark Yarhouse, the Hughes Endowed Chair and professor of psychology at Regent University in Virginia Beach, Virginia (a core faculty member in their doctoral program in clinical psychology), is the most prominent Christian researcher and clinician in this area. He established the Institute for the Study of Sexual Identity as a resource and research hub to deepen our compassionate understanding of gender dysphoria and sexual identity. The website for the ISSI, https://sexualidentityinstitute.org/, is a trustworthy resource for up-to-date information from a Christian perspective on struggles in this area. We recommend it enthusiastically.

# ABOUT THE AUTHORS

**STAN (STANTON L.) JONES, PHD,** is a clinical psychologist. He recently returned to serving as professor of psychology at Wheaton College after serving for twenty years as its provost (chief academic officer). Earlier, he led in establishing Wheaton's PsyD program in clinical psychology. He has been a visiting scholar at the University of Cambridge and has published many articles in journals such as *American Psychologist*, *General Psychologist*, *First Things*, and *Christianity Today*. Beyond the God's Design for Sex series, his books include *Psychology: A Student's Guide*, *Modern Psychotherapies: A Comprehensive Christian Appraisal* (2nd ed., with Richard E. Butman), *Ex-Gays?: A Longitudinal Study of Religiously Mediated Change in Sexual Orientation* (with Mark A. Yarhouse), and *Homosexuality: The Use of Scientific Research in the Church's Moral Debate* (with Mark A. Yarhouse).

**BRENNA JONES** serves in a professional ministry of discipleship and support as well as spiritual counsel and prayer for women. She served as a leader in a Bible-study ministry with women for a number of years. She has graduate training in biblical and theological studies.

**BRENNA AND STAN** wrote the original versions of their books on sex education while their three children were young; now they enjoy their three kids as adults, along with their kids' spouses and children.